Islamic Criminal Law in Nigeria

Islamic Criminal Law in Nigeria

Ruud Peters
(University of Amsterdam)

with the assistance of
Maarten Barends

Spectrum Books Limited
Ibadan
Abuja •Benin City •Lagos •Owerri

Spectrum titles can be purchased on line at
www.spectrumbooksonline.com

Published by
Spectrum Books Limited
Spectrum House
Ring Road
PMB 5612
Ibadan, Nigeria
e-mail: admin1@spectrumbooksonline.com

in association with
Safari Books (Export) Limited
1st Floor
17 Bond Street
St Helier
Jersey JE2 3NP
Channel Islands
United Kingdom

Europe and USA Distributor
African Books Collective Ltd
The Jam Factory
27 Park End Street
Oxford OX1, 1HU, UK

First published, 2003

ISBN: 978-029-421-X

Printed by: Evi-Coleman & Co.

Contents

Contents

Preface

This study is the outcome of a three-week assignment carried out on behalf of the European Commission by Ruud Peters, Professor of Islamic law, University of Amsterdam, assisted by Maarten Barends, a law student at the same University. Within the framework of the consultancy a two-week mission to Nigeria was conducted from 11 through 24 September 2001. Interviews were held in Lagos, Kano and Zaria (for the programme, see Appendix Two). Of crucial importance for this study was the assistance of Ms Marianne Nolte (Lagos), Civil Society Co-ordinator for the European Commission: We have greatly benefited from her contacts in Lagos and Kano as well as the necessary logistic support she offered us before and during our stay in Nigeria. The mission could not have been carried out without the assistance of Prof. Muhammad Tabi'u of the Faculty of Law, Bayero University Kano, who collected all the relevant legal texts and organised the four-day programme in Kano. The comments of Ms Asma'u Joda (Women Living Under Muslim Law) were very helpful. Finally we are very grateful to Ms Peri Bearman of Cambridge, MA, for her editorial comments.

The text of this published version differs on some points of detail from the original report submitted in September 2001. I have updated the text in the light of some Shari'a sentences issued during the past year, corrected a few minor omissions and inaccuracies and rewritten the section on the historical background. Moreover, in the light of the recent sentences to stoning on the strength of extramarital pregnancies, I have added some possible defences found in classical *Maliki* works of fiqh. The essence of the report and its conclusions have remained the same.

The aim of this study is to clarify and explain the circumstances and background of the recent introduction of Islamic criminal law in Northern Nigeria. In order to do so, a brief outline is given of Islamic Criminal Law (ICL) and its application in Northern Nigeria until the recent reintroduction of Shari'a law. Then the newly introduced Shari'a codes and their introduction will be analysed on the basis of the relevant legal texts (for a list of the consulted texts, see Appendix One) and on the basis of the interviews that we have conducted. A survey of the events connected with the introduction of Islamic criminal law and sentences pronounced under the new laws is presented in Appendix Two. In the subsequent chapters, constitutional problems and human rights issues connected with the introduction of Islamic criminal law will be discussed.

Chapter 1

Islamic Criminal Law: An overview

Classical Islamic law cannot be compared to a law code, but is rather an academic discourse of legal scholars, who often offer many contradictory interpretations of the revealed texts. There are four *Sunni* schools of jurisprudence,[1] each with its distinctive doctrine. The one prevailing in Northern Nigeria is the *Maliki* school and *Maliki* legal doctrine is the principal constituent of the Northern Nigerian legal practice. Therefore the *Maliki* school has been the basis for the following exposé.

What we call criminal law falls in the Shari'a under three separate headings:

- Qur'anic offences and their punishments (*hudûd*)
- The law of homicide and hurt
- Other crimes punishable at the discretion of the judge (*ta'zîr*, *siyâsa*)

The Qur'anic offences embody those which most engage non-Muslim attention. This domain, which has a certain symbolic function to present-day advocates of the reintroduction of the Shari'a, consists of crimes mentioned in the Qur'an, for which fixed penalties (*hudûd*, sing. *hadd*) are provided in the Shari'a. These are:

- Unlawful sexual intercourse (i.e. between persons who are not married), *zinâ*
- Theft, *sariqa*
- Robbery, *hirâba*
- Drinking of alcohol, *shurb al-khamr*
- False accusation of unlawful sexual intercourse, *qadhf*.

---

1. These are the *Maliki*, the *Hanafi*, the *Shafi'i* and the *Hanbali* schools; the *Shiite* school of jurisprudence has been left out of consideration

The fixed punishments for *zinâ* are stoning to death for persons who are currently married or have ever contracted a valid marriage. For those who have never contracted a marriage, the punishment is one hundred lashes and, in addition, banishment for men. **Theft** is to be punished by amputation of the right hand. **Robbery** is punished by death if a life has been taken, by death by crucifixion if both lives and property have been taken, by amputation of both the right hand and the left foot if only property has been taken, and by banishment if there was only a "hold up" without further aggravation. *Qadhf* and **drinking of alcohol** are both punishable with eighty lashes. An essential element with regard to the Qur'anic offences is that, if they are formally proven, the judge has no latitude in the choice of punishment.

The second domain, that of homicide and hurt, is one characterised by private prosecution in the sense that the culprit can only be sentenced and punished if the victim or his "avengers" demand punishment.[2] Whereas most Islamic jurists hold that the victim's heirs are his avengers, the *Maliki* school lays down that only the victim's adult, male, agnatic relatives (or in the absence of male agnates, his daughter or sister have this right (regardless of whether the victim was a man or a woman).

If homicide or hurt is committed intentionally, the punishment is retaliation (*qisâs*). Thus, for homicide the culprit may be punished by death, and for hurt causing the loss of limbs or senses, by inflicting the same injury on him, at least if this is technically possible without endangering the convict's life. Another condition is that the perpetrator's blood price must not exceed that of the victim, e.g. because of difference in religion.[3] If the death or the injury is not caused intentionally, or if the victim or his heirs are willing to forgo punishment "in kind",

---

2. There is one exception in Maliki law: treacherous killing (gatl ghila), i.e. luring someone away to a deserted spot in order to kill him, which can be punished with death regardless of the stance of the "avengers".
3. The blood price of a non-Muslim resident is one-half or one-third of that of a Muslim. Differences in blood price based on gender are not taken into consideration: a man can be sentenced to death for having killed a woman.

retaliation is then replaced by the payment of the blood price (*diya*). This is a fixed amount, and does not depend on a person's rank or wealth. The blood price for the killing of a free Muslim man is one hundred camels, one thousand dinars in gold or twelve thousand dirhams in silver. Women and non-Muslims have a lower value. For injuries, the classical books on law contain a tariff, according to which the amount of the blood price for a specific injury is given as a fraction of the blood price for homicide. In most cases, not the culprit but his *'âqila* (solidarity group, i.e. his tribe, or agnatic relatives) is obliged to pay the blood price.

The third domain of Islamic Criminal Law (ICL) has no clearly-defined offences. Judges have the discretionary power to punish sinful or otherwise undesirable acts. This is called *ta'zîr* or *siyâsa*. In the past, rulers often issued legislation in this field in order to restrict the freedom of the judges. In modern instances of codified Islamic criminal law we see the same. Usually the previously effective penal code is incorporated in the new criminal code and the offences and punishments mentioned therein are labelled *ta'zîr*.

The application of the severe punishments for the *hadd* offences is not free of obstacles. There are several reports according to which the Prophet Muhammad expressed his aversion of their application, and as a consequence, scholars have made the application difficult. The definitions of the *hadd* crimes are very strict and exclude many related acts that are equally undesirable. For example, the *hadd* punishment for theft (amputation of the right hand) can only be applied if the stolen goods have a certain minimum value (*nisâb*) and were taken from a locked or guarded place (*hirz*). Embezzlement, therefore, cannot be punished by the *hadd* penalty for theft. Moreover, with regard to the *hadd* crimes, the rules of evidence require either a confession, which may be withdrawn until the moment of the execution of the sentence, or the testimony of two (for unlawful sexual intercourse, four) male Muslim eye-witnesses of good reputation, who also may withdraw their testimonies until the moment of execution. Circumstantial evidence is not allowed for proving *hadd* crimes. However, there are two exceptions to this rule in *Maliki* doctrine. If a person reeks of alcohol, this is regarded as sufficient proof for the application of the *hadd* penalty for drinking of alcoholic beverages. The other, more consequential exception is that *Maliki* doctrine accepts as full evidence for unlawful sexual intercourse the pregnancy of a woman who is not married nor observing the waiting period (*'idda*) after the dissolution of her marriage.

In addition, the slightest doubt (*shubha*) prevents the application of the penalty. If a thief or someone who commits unlawful sexual intercourse had reasons to believe that he was entitled to take the property (e.g. a creditor with regard to the property of a debtor in arrears) or to have intercourse with the woman in question (e.g. because he thought he was married to her, whereas the marriage contract was void), then the fixed punishment cannot be imposed. Historical research with regard to the Ottoman Empire and nineteenth-century Egypt has shown that the mutilating *hadd* punishments were very seldom applied, if at all. This is also true for some countries where Islamic criminal law was introduced earlier than in Nigeria, such as Libya and Pakistan.

Since the *Maliki* doctrine that extramarital pregnancy constitutes full evidence of unlawful intercourse and may result in a sentence of stoning to death is followed by the Nigerian Shari'a courts, I will discuss here some possible defences found in the standard *Maliki* legal texts. A woman who is accused of unlawful sexual intercourse (*zinâ*) on the strength of her pregnancy has essentially three defences based on doubt (*shubha*). If she was married before and the pregnancy occurred after the expiry of the waiting period, she may claim that the child was nevertheless fathered by her former husband, since *Maliki* doctrine recognises the possibility of pregnancies lasting four or seven years, a phenomenon called "the sleeping foetus".[4]

---

4. The following text taken from al-Dardir's commentary on Khalil's Mukhtasar, one of the most authoritative works of the Maliki madhhab, makes this clear: "If a woman during her waiting period (*'idda*) is not sure whether or not she is pregnant, she must wait the maximum period of gestation which is according to some scholars five years and according to others four. [The author al-Dazuqi inserts a gloss here to the effect that other *Maliki* authorities claim that the maximum period of gestation is six or seven years].(...) If such a woman marries four months before the five years have lapsed and gives birth five months after her first sexual contact with her new

Another defence is that she claims that intercourse took place without penetration ("between her thighs"), but that the sperm entered her vagina. Since penetration is an essential element of the definition of *zinâ*, this constitutes sufficient uncertainty to avert the application of the *hadd* penalty[5]. Finally she may claim that the pregnancy must be the result of sexual intercourse that took place during her sleep without her knowing it[6]. For the two last defences she does not have to produce evidence (The texts state clearly: *tuqbal da'wâhâ*, i.e. her claim is accepted). The defence that she has been raped is different in this respect. *Maliki* doctrine requires for this plea to be accepted that there be circumstantial evidence, e.g. testimonies to the effect that she came to her village or family while being upset and screaming that she had been raped, or with torn clothes or covered with blood as a result of fighting.

The enforcement of the Shari'a in Northern Nigeria: Historical background[7]

The Shari'a has always been an essential element of the legal system of Northern Nigeria. When the British occupied Northern

---

husband, neither the first nor the second husband is regarded as the father, for with regard to the first one, the delivery took place one month after the five years [the maximum period of gestation], whereas regarding the second, because she gave birth within six months [the minimum period of gestation ending with childbirth]. She must be punished with the *hadd* penalty because it is certain that the child was begotten in unlawful intercourse. [Al-Dasuqi adds here that the *hadd* punishment should not be applied since there is uncertainty, as it has been related on the authority of Malik that the maximum period of gestation is six or seven years]. See l-Dasuqi, Hashiyat al-Dasuqi ala al-Sharh al-Kabir li-l-Dardir. Cairo: Isa al-Babi al-Halabi, n.d., ii, 474. (Chapter: A free woman observes a waiting period of..."

5. See Ibn Farhun, Tabsirat al-hukkam (Cairo, 1986), ii, 97 (Ch. 64 on giving judgement on zina on the strength of evidence of pregnancy).

6. See Al-Sawi, Hashiyat al-Sawi 'ala al-Sharh al-Saghir (Cairo, Dar al-Ma'arif, n.d.), iv, p.455. Ch. Proving zina (Thubut al-zina),

7. This chapter is based on E.H. Ofori-Amankwah,. Criminal Law in the Northern States of Nigeria. (Zaria, Gaskiya Corporation: 1986), pp. 52-59; A. Aguda I. Okagbue, Principles of Criminal Liability in Nigerian Law. (Ibadan: Heinemann Educational Books Nigeria, 1991), pp.7-17, 30-36; F.E.O. Ume. The Courts and Administration of Law in Nigeria. (Enugu: Fourth Dimension Publishers, 1989), pp.70-83; J.N.D. Anderson. Islamic Law in Africa. (London: H.M.'s Stationery Office, 1954), pp.171-224; J. M.Abun-Nasr. "The recognition of Islamic law in Nigeria as customary law: its justifications and consequences." *Law, Society and National Identity in Africa.* Ed. J.M. Abu-Nasr a.o (Hamburg: Buske Verlag, 1990)

Nigeria, they allowed that ICL according to the *Maliki* school continued to be applied, like many other systems of customary law, and interfered with and influenced its application only on those points that they regarded as being repugnant to "natural justice, equity and good conscience". Except for the ban on mutilating penalties and stoning to death there were, to the best of my knowledge, no British objections to the application of ICL until the end of the 1940s. After that time, British interference was limited to capital offences and certain procedural rules.

When the British occupied Northern Nigeria, they left the local emirs in their positions of power. They intended to exert control through the existing administrative and judicial structures. The Native Court Proclamation of 1900 was based on this principle: The British Resident (provincial governor) could establish, with the emir's consent, native courts with full jurisdiction in civil and criminal matters over the native population. Thus the existing courts of the emirs and the alkalis were given official status in the new British colonial order. The judges were appointed by the emirs, with the approval of the Residents. They were to apply native law and custom, i.e. *Maliki* Islamic law. They could award any type of punishment, except mutilation and torture or any other which was repugnant to humanity and natural justice. The British Resident, however, had extensive powers to supervise and control the courts: he could enter and inspect the courts, suspend, reduce and modify sentences or order a rehearing of the trial before another native court or a transfer to a provincial court (i.e. a court applying English common law).[8] In an address given in the Northern

pp. 31-45; I.O. reflection." *Nigerian Law Journal* vol.5 (1971), pp. 119-128; M. Tabi'u. "Constraints in the Application of Islamic Law in Nigeria." *Islamic Law in Nigeria: Application and Teaching*. Ed. S.K. Rashid. (Lagos etc.: Islamic Publications Bureau, 1986), pp. 75-85; S.Kumo. "The Application of Islamic Law in Northern Nigeria: Problems and Prospects." *Islamic law in Nigeria: Application and Teaching*. Ed. S.K. Rashidi. (Lagos etc.: Islamic Publications Bureau 1986), pp.42-51.

8. E.A. Keay and S.S. Richardson, *The Native and Customary Courts of Nigeria* (London etc.: Sweet & Maxwell, 1966). pp.20-2.

town of Sokoto in 1902, the British Governor-General Lord Lugard described his policy as follows:

> The alkalis and emirs will hold the Law Courts as of old, but bribes are forbidden, and mutilation and confinement of men in inhuman prisons are not lawful. (…) Sentences of death will not be carried out without the consent of the Resident. (…) Every person has the right to appeal to the Resident who will, however, endeavour to uphold the power of the Native Courts to deal with native cases according to the law and the custom of the country.[9]

The Native Courts Proclamation was changed several times before it was replaced by the native Courts Ordinance of 1933. These changes introduced a hierarchy of courts and a system of appeal within the native courts system, and beyond that to the Nigerian High (later, Supreme) Court and to the newly created West African Court of Appeal. In hearing cases of Islamic law, these Courts of Appeal would be assisted by Muslim jurists. The system of supervision and control by British administrative officials was continued with changes on points of detail.[10]

From the beginning, the native courts had full jurisdiction in criminal cases, except that capital sentences – the emir's courts, the highest in the hierarchy, had the power to pronounce these — had to be approved by the Governor after review by the Resident. When in 1904 a Criminal Code was introduced in Northern Nigeria, Shari'a criminal law was not abolished. Section 4 of this code stipulated: "No person shall be liable to be tried or punished in any court in Nigeria, other than a native tribunal, for an offence except under the express provisions of the Code or some other Ordinance or some law (…)." This section exempted the native courts from the principle that criminal sentences had to be founded on statute law and allowed to try acts under Islamic law (*qua* customary law), regardless of

---

9. A.G Karibi-Whyte, *History and Sources of Nigerian Criminal Law, Spectrum Law Series* (Ibadan: Spectrum Law Pub., 1993). p.177.
10.Keay and Richardson, *The Native and Customary Courts of Nigeria.* pp.25-44

whether or not they were punishable under the Criminal Code and even in the case that the offence was known under the Criminal Code. Therefore, they would convict persons for illegal sexual intercourse (*zinâ*), which is an offence under Islamic law, but not under the 1904 Criminal Code.

The application of Islamic law by the native courts in the North extended to the courts' practice and procedure. The British authorities gave these courts much latitude. In a 1930 decision, the West African Court of Appeal recognised the *Maliki qasâma* procedure, on the strength of which a suspect against whom there is some but not sufficient evidence, can be sentenced to death if the victim's male next of kin swear fifty oaths against him. The Emir of Katsina's court had found a certain Abdullah Kogi guilty of wilful homicide, although there was no admission nor any eyewitnesses, nor other evidence that could show that he had committed the offence. There was however circumstantial evidence (*lawth*) to support the conviction. Therefore, the West African Court of Appeal sent the case back and instructed the Emir's court to look for the victim's relatives to swear a *qasâma* oath, in order to make the sentence lawful. The Court of Appeal explained its position as follows:

> There is no desire to interfere with decisions which are in accordance with native law, the principle has b that the verdict and sentence of a Native Court wl an integral part of our judicial system carried out in accordance with procedure enjoined by native law and not obviously inequitable will be accepted even though the procedure is widely different from the practice of English Criminal Courts.[11]

I have found only one decision in which an aspect of the Islamic law of procedure was declared to be repugnant to natural justice, equity and good conscience. This was the rule that in

---

11. Abdullahi Kogi & others vs Katsina Native Authority (1930) 14 NLR 49 as quoted in A.G. Karibi-Whyte, History and Sources of Nigerian Criminal Law, Spectrum Law Series (Ibadan: Spectrum Law Publication, 1993). See also Abdulmalik Bappa Mahmud. A brief history of Shari'ah in the defunct Northern Nigeria, [S.I.: s.n., 1988. p.18

the trial of $hadd crimes, if the plaintiff produces full evidence, the defendant is not permitted to put forward a defence. In this case, the Emir of Hadejia's Court found a man called Guri guilty of homicide while attempting to rob and therefore sentenced him to death. On appeal, the Federal Supreme Court annulled the judgement on the ground that the appellant was not allowed to defend himself. This is because according to the Islamic law of evidence, an accused is not allowed to give evidence on his behalf, while under English law, he can do so, but in a witness box. The court held that this rule of procedure and evidence of Islamic law was repugnant to natural justice, equity and good conscience.[12]

Under the wording of Section 4 of the Criminal Code of 1904 (vide supra), the nearly unlimited jurisdiction of Native Courts to administer Islamic criminal justice was clearly established. In 1933, however, this section 4 was amended. The phrase "other than a native tribunal" was deleted and the wording became: "No person shall be liable to be tried or punished in any court in Nigeria for an offence except under the express provisions of the Code or some other Ordinance or some law (...)." Initially judicial practice did not change. The common interpretation of "some other Ordinance" was that it referred to the Native Court Ordinance, which expressly permitted criminal proceedings under native law and custom (and thus under Islamic law).[13] However, a 1947 decision of the West Africa Court of Appeal changed this. The Court of Appeal quashed a capital sentence pronounced by the Emir of Gwandu's court, since the offence for which the accused had been convicted, wilful homicide, justified the sentence according to Islamic law, but was not a capital offence under the Criminal Code.[14] In this case the

---

12. Guri vs Hadejia Native Authority (1959) 4 FSC 44. Abdulmalik Bappa Mahmud. A brief history of Shari'a in the defunct Northern Nigeria, (S.l.: s.n., 1988) p.17.

13. The Native Court Ordinance of 1933 (S.10(2)) laid down in this regard: "Native courts (...) may impose a fine or imprisonment(...) or may inflict any punishment authorised by native law or custom provided it does not involve mutilation or torture, and is not repugnant to natural justice and humanity."

14. As summarised in Muhammad Tabi'u. "Constraints in the Application of Islamic Law in Nigeria." In *Islamic Law in Nigeria: Application and Teaching*, edited by S. Khalid Rashid. Lagos etc.: Islamic Publications Bureau, 1986. Pp. 75-85.

accused was sentenced to death for having killed a man who had a relationship with his wife. The emir's court had not accepted the defence that the homicide had been justified, arguing that that would only be the case if his life had been threatened. The Court of Appeal ruled that the accused had acted under provocation and that his act was therefore to be qualified as manslaughter, which under the Criminal Code is not a capital offence.[15] This decision gave rise to much confusion. A common interpretation of it was that the Native Courts in the North could apply ICL only if there was no specific provision in the Criminal Code, and that otherwise the Native Courts had to give their sentences on the basis of the Criminal Code.[16] This gave rise to consternation protests from the Islamic judges, who considered the new interpretation as an unwarranted intrusion upon their jurisdiction to administer ICL.[17] This resulted in an amendment of the Native Courts Ordinance, to the effect that where the same act amounted to an offence under a written law and under a customary law, the maximum punishment that could be given in a trial by a native court was the one prescribed by the written law. The basic principle applied here was that guilt would be established under native law and that subsequently the court should turn to the Criminal Code for guidance on the sentence. This provision was difficult to apply, since the *alkalis* were not familiar with the Criminal Code. For this reason, the Supreme Court could in appeal quash or reverse capital sentences for homicide pronounced by Islamic courts, even in the original sentence was correct according to *Maliki* law.[18]

The tension between ICL and British notions of justice became manifest first and foremost in the trying of homicide cases. After a period of nearly five decades during which the Native Courts could apply the *Maliki* doctrine of homicide without restrictions,

---

15. Tsofo Gunna v. Gwandu Native Authority (1947) 12 W.A.C.A. 141, as summarised in Abdulmalik Bappa Mahmud. A brief history of Sharia in the defunct Northern Nigeria, Pp.17-8.
16. Karibi-Whyte, *History and Sources of Nigerian Criminal Law*. p.165.
17. Keay and Richardson, *The Native and Customary Courts of Nigeria*. pp.48-9; Karibi-Whyte, *History and Sources of Nigerian Criminal Law*. p.165.
18. Karibi-Whyte, *History and Sources of Nigerian Criminal Law*. pp.182-7

the differences came to the surface after 1948. The main problem was that under ICL, manslaughter (wilful killing) is a capital offence. Whereas under the 1904 Criminal Code, killing incurred the death penalty only if carried out with premeditation (murder). Moreover, the idea of private justice was also a thorn in the flesh of the British jurists. If in cases of wilful homicide no sentence of retaliation could be pronounced, e.g. because the victim's next of kin waived their right to demand the killer's death, and only the blood price was due, the killer, according to Maliki doctrine, would be sentenced to one year imprisonment and one hundred lashes. As a result, offenders could be sentenced to death for homicide which would constitute only manslaughter, not a capital offence under the Criminal Code. On the other hand, those guilty of premeditated homicide might be sentenced to only one year imprisonment if the victim's next of kin did not demand his death, or if there was some other bar to capital punishment, such as the fact that the victim was the killer's offspring or a Christian. In such cases, British law prevailed after 1948.

In cases of wounding no sentences of retaliation would be imposed, usually with the argument that such wounds could not be inflicted without endangering the life of the convict. Instead the culprit would be sentenced to pay financial compensation (*diya, arsh, hukûma*) in addition to imprisonment or a fine. However, if a court would have sentenced an offender to retaliation, the sentence, constitution mutilation, would have been commuted to imprisonment.

The laws of $hadd were faithfully enforced, except, as we have seen, that sentences of amputation or stoning to death would not be carried out and be commuted into imprisonment. Caning and flogging were also lawful punishments, but sentences imposing these penalties had to be confirmed by the Emir or the District Officer.[19] There were different kinds of flogging. Flogging imposed as a $hadd punishment (*"haddi lashing"*) had to be administered with a cowhide whip, by someone holding some object under his arm, so as to prevent the use of his full strength.

19.Native Court Ordinance 1933 s.16.

The punishment consisted in the disgrace rather than in the physical suffering.[20] The penalty of flogging would, for women, be commuted to imprisonment or a fine. As a result of the restrictions concerning punishment, the distinction between $hadd theft and other forms of theft had been obliterated. For robbery (*hirâba*) the same applied as for theft, except when someone had been killed during the robbery, in which case the Emir's court could sentence the accused to capital punishment, applying the pertinent rules of the Shari'a. With regard to illegal sexual intercourse, the *Maliki* rule was applied that women could be convicted on the basis of extramarital pregnancy (unless such a woman could prove that she had been forced). Unfounded allegation of illegal sexual intercourse (*qadhf*) and drinking of alcohol (*shurb al-khamr*) were usually punished with eighty lashes or a fine.

The direct but controlled and restricted application of Islamic criminal law came to an end in 1960 when the new Penal Code Law for the Northern Region 1959 was brought into effect. This Code remained in force until the recent enactment of Shari'a Criminal Codes. The Penal Code of 1959 was based on the Indian (1860) and the Sudanese (1899) Penal Codes, and was essentially an English code. However, here and there special provisions were included based on Shari'a Criminal Law. Thus illegal sexual intercourse (S. 387-388) and drinking of alcohol (S. 403) remained punishable by law for Muslims. However, only S. 403 explicitly applies to Muslims, the other sections only to men or women "subject to any customary law in which extra-marital intercourse is recognised as a criminal offence". Moreover, Muslim offenders could be sentenced, in addition to the penalties prescribed by the law, to "haddi lashing" (see above), for the $hadd offences of unlawful sexual intercourse, defamation (if constituting the $hadd offence of *qadhf*) and drinking of alcohol. (S. 68(2) This type of corporal punishment is intended to deter by the public disgrace involved, rather than by the pain.

20.Alan Gledhill, *The Penal Codes of Northern Nigeria and the Sudan, Law in Africa; No.8* (London: Sweet & Maxwell, 1963). pp.768-9.

Chapter 2

The Reintroduction of Shari'a Criminal Law

Introduction

On 27 January 2000 Zamfara State enacted the first Shari'a Penal Code in Northern Nigeria. Shari'a courts had already been established earlier. All this was regarded by many as a political move by Zamfara's governor, Ahmed Sani, to enhance his popular support. The example of Zamfara was followed in May by Niger State, where the government, like that in Zamfara, fully supported the re-Islamisation of the legal system. Other Northern states,[1] prompted by popular pressure, followed suit. In Katsina and Sokoto Shari'a criminal sentences were pronounced and executed (in one case amputation of the right hand was applied)[2] even before the introduction of a Shari'a Penal Code, on the strength of Shari'a Courts Laws stipulating that the Shari'a courts must apply the provisions of the Qur'an and *Hadîth* (sayings and acts of the Prophet Muhammad) and those found in the traditional authoritative *Maliki* works of law.

So far, twelve Northern states have introduced Shari'a criminal law by setting up Shari'a courts with jurisdiction in criminal matters. Borno, Gombe, Kaduna and Katsina are reportedly (by the end of 2001) still in the process of preparing Shari'a penal codes. I have not been able to consult the relevant bills. Seven states (Bauchi, Jigawa, Kano, Kebbi, Sokoto, Yobe and Zamfara) have introduced Shari'a criminal law by enacting

---

1. Bauchi (June 2001), Jigawa (during 2000), Kano (November 2000), Kebbi (December 2000), Sokoto (January 2001) and Yobe (April 2001).
2. Katsina: Two sentences for unlawful sexual intercourse, lashing for the woman and lashing with imprisonment for the man, in the town of Malunfashi (15 and 16) November 2000); sentences for drinking alcohol (9 March 2001); also in Malunfashi, Ahmed Tijani was sentenced to have his right eye removed after blinding a man in an assault. The victim of the assault could choose between retaliation ('an eye for an eye') and 50 camels (26 May 2001).
   Sokoto: The punishment of amputation of the right hand was carried out on a person for having stolen a goat and ₦6,000 (7 July 2001); sentence of amputation of the right hand pronounced for the stealing of car parts worth $152 (1 July 2001)

13

completely new penal codes. With the exception of the Kano Penal Code, these penal codes are almost identical copies of the Zamfara Penal Code, the first to be enacted.[3] One state (Niger) has only amended the 1960 Penal Code to bring it into agreement with the Shari'a by adding S. 68A summarising the law of Qur'anic offences (*hudûd*), homicide and hurt.

The reintroduction of Shari'a criminal law is in the first place justified on religious grounds. Many Muslims believe that in order to be good Muslims they must live in an Islamic order, enforced by the state. They argue that the establishment of such an order is warranted under S. 38 of the Constitution, guaranteeing freedom of religious practice. In addition, many Muslims welcome the implementation of Islamic criminal law on practical grounds: they see it as a panacea against a wide range of social evils, such as soaring crime rates and corruption. Islamic criminal law, with its harsh punishments for homicide, grievous hurt, theft, robbery and immoral behaviour, is regarded as an adequate answer. For the same reason, most Northern state legislators have introduced the possibility of imposing corporal punishment (caning) for many other offences, considering that the deterrent effect of such punishment is greater than fining or imprisonment. Furthermore, the Islamic judicial system is seen as one that dispenses fast justice, not attaching too great a value to procedural technicalities.

None of the laws was introduced with an explanatory memorandum, clarifying and justifying the provisions and the choices that were made during the legislative process. They all seem to have been drafted in great haste. This explains the poor legislative quality of the codes with lapses such as faulty, sometimes even incomprehensible wording, incorrect cross references, omissions and contradictions. In a number of instances it seems that incomplete wording or omissions were included deliberately, as the legislators foresaw constitutional problems. This, for example, could be why in a number of penal codes the requirements of proof with regard to the Qur'anic

---

3. The differences between the Kano Penal Code and the other penal codes are mainly a matter of arrangement and many of the sections are a verbatim copy of the other.

punishments have been omitted in clear recognition of the fact that the law of evidence is a federal matter (see Chapter 3). Another factor that may have contributed to the deficiencies in the codes was the feeling that the law itself was no more than an instrument to introduce Islamic criminal law and that in cases in which the law was not clear or silent, recourse could be had to the traditional texts of *Maliki* legal doctrine.

Introduction of Shari'a Penal Codes has not put an end to the direct enforcement of uncodified Islamic criminal law, for most of these codes contain articles stipulating that:

> any act or omission which is not specifically mentioned in this Shari'a Penal Code but is otherwise declared to be an offence under the Qur'an, *Sunnah* and *Ijtihad* of the *Maliki* School of Islamic thought shall be an offence under this code and such act or omission shall be punishable:

(a)   With imprisonment for a term which may extend to 5 years, or
(b)   With caning which may extend to 50 lashes, or
(c)   With fine which may extend to ₦5,000.00 or with any two of the above punishments.[4]

There now seems to be a general awareness among Muslim lawyers of the North that the Shari'a Penal Codes that have thus far been enacted are of poor legislative quality. In the year 2001, the Institute for Islamic Legal Studies of Ahmadu Bello University in Zaria, has initiated a project with federal backing to work together with representatives of the relevant states, Islamic scholars and common law jurists to prepare a unified penal code for the North. Its immediate aim is to introduce one single Shari'a Penal Code which will be widely applied. It is expected that this will enhance legal certainty and facilitate the training of judicial staff and police personnel. Moreover, the project aims at redressing the poor drafting. Among those involved in the project are jurists who would like to emphasise

---

4. See e.g. Zamfara Penal Code, S.92; Jigawa Penal Code, S.92; Bauchi Penal Code, S.95; Yobe Penal Code, S.92; Kebbi Penal Code, S.93; Sokoto Penal Code, S.94

the restrictions and limitations that would make the application of the severe Qur'anic punishments more difficult. At the moment, it is difficult to say how much weight their views carry, but it is clear that they deserve support.

Changes in the judiciary

All states that reintroduced Shari'a criminal law have made changes in the judicial set-up. Before the Islamisation, there were two sets of courts in the North:

- Magistrate courts applying common law, with the High Court as appellate court.
- Area courts (also known as *alkalis'* courts), on three levels, applying the Shari'a in civil and the 1960 Penal Code in criminal cases.

In matters of personal law (marriage, succession etc.), appeal from decisions by area courts was open, according to S. 275-277 of the Constitution, to the Shari'a Courts of Appeal. In all other matters, regardless of whether or not Islamic law had been applied, the High Court was the appellate court.

The Islamisation of the legal system brought changes to this system. The area courts were henceforth called Shari'a Courts (with Upper Shari'a Courts and Higher Shari'a Courts) and were to adjudicate according to the Shari'a. Since the Constitution enjoins that criminal law must be codified, the Shari'a Courts laws of most states contain a provision that the state legislator shall enact a criminal code and a code of criminal procedure.

These new Shari'a Courts have jurisdiction in all civil litigation if both parties are Muslim, and in criminal proceedings if the accused is a Muslim. The jurisdiction of the Shari'a Courts may extend to non-Muslims if they voluntarily accept this jurisdiction in a specific proceeding.

A further measure was that the jurisdiction of the Shari'a Court of Appeal of the state was extended to all civil and criminal cases tried before the Lower Shari'a Courts. As we shall see this extension of jurisdiction has raised some constitutional questions. According to the Constitution, appeal to the Federal Court of

Appeal from judgements of the State Shari'a Courts of Appeal is only open in cases involving Muslim personal law (S. 244(1)). One practical consequence is that if by virtue of state legislation, these Shari'a Courts of Appeal were to hear other cases as well, these judgements would be final and constitutional if there is no possibility to challenge them.

The Shari'a Court laws stipulate that its judges must be learned in Islamic law and they define their qualifications. Most of the, laws create institutions or offices to advise, supervise and control the functioning of the Shari'a Courts (e.g. a council of '*ulama*', judicial inspectors, muftis) or assign such powers to existing officials (such as the Grand Kadi, i.e. the president of the Shari'a Court of Appeal).

The Shari'a Courts shall sit in an open place, to which members of the public shall have access. Regulations shall be enacted for *in camera* sessions. Persons charged with criminal offences are entitled to defend themselves in person or by a legal practitioner of their choice.

We heard many complaints that the changes were not properly introduced. The judges of the new Shari'a Courts were the same judges who had sat in the area courts, but they had not been prepared nor trained to apply the changes in the legal system. Ignorance of the law of procedure, we were told, seriously hampered the course of justice.

Analysis of the codes

The Shari'a Penal Codes enacted in Northern Nigeria follow the models of earlier codifications of Islamic criminal law, introduced elsewhere in the Islamic world.[5] This means that they are amendments to the previously effective penal codes. Added are:

- Provisions on the Qur'anic offences (*hudûd*)
- Provisions on homicide and hurt
- Corporal punishment (caning or flogging) as a penalty for many other offences

---

5. See Peters, R. "The Islamization of Criminal Law: a comparative analysis." *Welt des Islams* 34, No.ii (1994): 246-274

In the following, the Zamfara Penal Code (adopted also by Bauchi, Jigawa, Kebbi, Sokoto and Yobe), the Kano Penal Code and the Niger State amendments will be analysed. I will highligh those points where the codes contain contradictory provision or deviate from classical *Maliki* doctrine.

Punishments
The section listing the punishments[6] introduces the new Shari'a penalties:
- retaliation (for homicide and grievous hurt)
- death by stoning
- amputation of the right hand or the right hand and left foot
- caning
- blood-wit (or blood price, *diya*), as a compensation for homicide and hurt

In most codes the list is not exhaustive, as other punishments are mentioned in the sections on offences. The Zamfara Penal Code, for instance, does not list death by stoning and crucifixion in S. 93, which enumerates the punishments that are allowed under the Code. Nevertheless these penalties are mentioned in Sections 127(b) and 153 (d). S. 93 also lists such "punishments" as reprimand, public disclosure, boycott and exhortation. These, however, are not mentioned in the sections on special offences.

The Qur'anic offences punishable by lashing
The rules with regard to the Qur'anic offences (*hudûd*) follow on the whole the classical *Maliki* doctrine. Drinking of alcohol is made punishable by eighty lashes (Niger State: either forty or eighty, without indication as to the grounds on which the number of lashes is selected) and the manufacturing, storing, trading etc. of alcohol by forty lashes and/or a maximum of six months' imprisonment.[7] In addition, the Kano Penal Code (S. 136(2)) makes the use of drugs ("taking, injecting or inhaling any substance for the purpose of intoxication") punishable by

---

6. Zamfara Penal Code, S.93; Kano Penal Code, S.92
7. Kano Penal Code, S. 136(1), 137; Zamfara Penal Code. S. 149-150; Niger State Penal Code, S. 68A (2) (e).

eighty lashes and/or a maximum of one year imprisonment. False accusation of unlawful sexual intercourse (*qadhf*) is made punishable by eighty lashes.[8]

Unlawful sexual intercourse (zinâ)

Unlawful sexual intercourse (*zinâ*) is to be punished by death by stoning if the offender is married or has ever been married. In other cases the penalty is one hundred lashes. Men are, in addition, punished by imprisonment for one year.[9] Sodomy (defined as intercourse by penetration in the rectum of a man or woman) is regarded as *zinâ* and punished in the same way.[10]

Rape is regarded as a special case of *zinâ* and is made punishable by the same punishments, except that the Kano Penal Code, following the 1960 Penal Code, extends the imprisonment for the rapist to life.[11] The Kano and Zamfara Penal Codes also oblige the perpetrator to pay compensation up to the amount of the proper bride price. The fact that rape is assimilated to *zinâ* puts women at a great disadvantage because in principle both parties to *zinâ* are liable to punishment. If a woman reports to the police that she is a victim of rape, this can easily be construed as a confession to unlawful intercourse which makes her liable to the *hadd* punishment, unless she can prove that intercourse took place without her consent. The burden of proof in that case is hers. Moreover, if her attacker does not confess, her accusations against him amount to defamation (*qadhf*, unfounded allegation of unlawful sexual intercourse), for which she can be punished by an additional eighty lashes.

According to classical *Maliki* doctrine, the pregnancy of an unmarried woman is proof of *zina*. Although the new Penal Codes are silent on this point, this rule was applied in a case tried in a Zamfara court. In September 2000, a pregnant seventeen

---

8. Kano Penal Code, S.130-31; Zamfara Penal Code, S. 139-41; Niger State Penal Code, S. 68A (2) (d).
9. Kano Penal Code, S. 125. Zamfara Penal Code, S. 127 does not stipulate that the imprisonment is only for men; Niger Penal Code (S. 68 (2) (c) does not mention imprisonment at all.
10. Kano Penal Code, S. 128-29; Zamfara Penal Code, S. 130-31
11. Kano Penal Code, S. 126-27; Zamfara Penal Code, S.128-29

year old girl, Bariya Ibrahim Magazu, was found guilty of pre-marital sex and was sentenced to 180 lashes, to be administered on 27 January 2001, at least 40 days after she had had her baby. The number of lashes is composed of one hundred for *zina* and eighty for defamation. On 13 January 2001 the execution of Bariya Ibrahim Magazu's sentence was postponed and reduced to one hundred lashes as she was no longer found guilty of defamation (*qadhf*), apparently having withdrawn her claims against the three men for lack of evidence. The sentence was carried out in public on 22 January 2001.

Both the Kano[12] and Niger[13] Penal Codes lay down that *zinâ* (including rape) can only be proven by confession or four witnesses (Kano: four male or eight female witnesses). The Zamfara Penal Code is silent in this respect. By now it has become clear that the Shari'a courts follow the *Maliki* doctrine according to which extramarital pregnancy is also regarded as full evidence for *zinâ*. In September 2000 a pregnant girl, Bariya Ibrahim Magazu, an unmarried pregnant girl, whose age was reported as seventeen by official and thirteen by many other sources, was found guilty of pre-marital sex and was sentenced by a Zamfara Shari'a court to 180 lashes, to be administered on 27 January 2001, at least 40 days after she had had her baby. The number of lashes is composed of one hundred for *zinâ* and eighty for defamation. On 13 January 2001 the execution of Bariya Ibrahim Magazu's sentence was postponed and reduced to one hundred lashes as she was no longer found guilty of defamation (*qadhf*), apparently having withdrawn her claims against the three men for lack of evidence. The sentence was carried out in public on 22 January 2001, before the expiration of forty days period after delivery. Two more cases of this kind have been tried. On 9 October 2001, Safiya Hussaini Tungar-Tudu was sentenced to death by stoning by the Upper Shari'a Court in Gwadabawa, Sokoto State, for *zinâ* proven by her extramarital pregnancy. On 25 March 2002, however, the verdict was quashed on technical grounds, the most important of which was that the code under

---

12. Kano Penal Code, S. 127, Explanation; Code of Criminal Procedure, S. 396
13. Niger Penal Code, S. 68A (3) (b).

which she had been sentenced was not yet in force when she had committed the alleged offence. Amina Lawal in Katsina State has, as yet, not been so fortunate. On 18 August 2002, the Upper Shari'a Court of Funtua upheld the decision of a lower Shari'a court sentencing her to be stoned. The sentence is not to be carried out before early 2004, taking into account the maximum period of two years during which a mother is supposed to nurse her child. Her lawyers have announced that they will appeal the verdict. These sentences are unconstitutional on several counts. The evidence on which they were based discriminates against women, since men, for the same offence, can only be condemned on the strength of a confession or the testimony of four witnesses. This is in conflict with Section 42(1) of the constitution. Moreover, the evidence is unlawful in view of the fact that the law of evidence is a federal matter. And finally, stoning must be regarded as a cruel, degrading and inhuman punishment, prohibited in Section 34(1). (See also Ch. 6)

Theft (*sariqa*)

The provisions in the new Shari'a Codes regarding theft, for which the *hadd* punishment of amputation of the right hand from the wrist[14] is incurred, are also very similar to classical *Maliki* doctrine. The Kano and Zamfara Penal Codes[15] define it as

> covertly, dishonestly and without consent taking any lawful and movable property belonging to another, out of its place of custody (*hirz*) and valued not less than the minimum stipulated value (*nisâb*) without any justification.

The minimum stipulated value (*nisâb*) is defined as a "minimum amount of property (...) which, if stolen, shall attract *hadd* punishment,"[16] a circular definition which is not of great

---

14. The Kano (S.134) and Zamfara (S.145) Penal Codes stipulate that in the event of subsequent recidivism the left foot, the left hand and the right foot will be amputated.
15. Kano Penal Code, S.133; Zamfara Penal Code, S.144
16. Zamfara Penal Code, S.46; Kano Penal Code, S.46.

help for a legal practitioner. In classical *Maliki* law the amount was precisely defined in terms of gold and silver.[17] If the *nisâb* is not assigned a monetary value, this may result in legal uncertainty, especially since so much depends on its definition. In a judgement pronounced on 7 July 2001, a Sokoto Shari'a court presided by judge Bawa Sahabi Tambuwal, fixed the *nisâb* at 869 Naira (ca. US$ 8), which seems to be rather low. The Niger State Penal Code (S. 68A (2)(a)) does not adopt the Shari'a definition, but refers to the sections on theft of the 1960 Penal Code (S. 287-290) and stipulates that the stolen goods must have a minimum value of 20,000 Naira (about US$150 by the end of 2001) and must have been stolen from proper custody.

The Kano (S. 135) and Zamfara (S. 147) Penal Codes (but not the Niger amendment) also list eight defence pleas that under classical *Maliki* law preclude the application of the penalty of amputation.[18] If such pleas are accepted, the offender will be punished by imprisonment not exceeding one year and by fifty lashes.

In some codes certain offences are equated with theft and can also be punished by amputation. Most Penal Codes make the kidnapping of a child under seven (or before puberty in some

---

17. About one gram of gold (one quarter of a dinar of 4,25 grams) or about nine grams of silver (3 dirhams of ca. 3 grams).

18. "The penalty of *hadd* for theft shall be remitted in any of the following cases:-

(a) Where the offence was committed by ascendant against descendant;

(b) Where the offence was committed between spouses within their matrimonial home; provided the stolen property was not under the victim's lock and key;

(c) Where the offence was committed under circumstances of necessity and the offender did not take more than he ordinarily requires to satisfy his need or the need of his dependents;

(d) Where the offender believes in good faith that he has a share (or a right or interest) in the said stolen property and the said stolen property does not exceed the share (or the right or interest) to the equivalent of the minimum value of the property (*nisâb*);

(e) Where the offender retracts his confession before execution of the penalty in cases where proof of guilt was based only on the confession of the offender;

(f) Where the offender returns or restitutes the stolen property to the victim of the offence and repents before he was brought to trial, he being a first time offender;

(g) Where the offender was permitted access to the place of custody (hirz) of the stolen property;

(h) Where the victim of the offence is indebted to the offender and is unwilling to pay, and the debt was due to be discharged prior to the offence, and the value of the property stolen is equal to, or does not exceed the debt due to the offender to the extent of the *nisâb*." (*Zamfara Penal Code, S. 147*)

codes) punishable by amputation.[19] The Zamfara Penal Code (S. 259) has a clause imposing amputation as the penalty for forgery of documents if the value they represent is more than the *nisâb*. The Kano Penal Code has also made embezzlement of public funds or of funds of a bank or company by officials and employees an offence punishable by amputation (S. 134B). The wording of the section (here quoted verbatim) is not very clear:

> Whoever is a public servant or a staff of a private sector including bank or company connives with somebody or some other people or himself and stole public funds or property under his care or somebody under his jurisdiction, he shall be punished with amputation of his right hand wrist (...).

To the best of my knowledge, such offences do not fall under the definition of theft according to classical doctrine and cannot be regarded as a *hadd* crime. Some classical *Maliki* authorities regard this as a lawful punishment for the offence on the basis of *ta'zîr*. Another dangerous development is that the defence arguments for theft, a critical constituent of this part of the law, do not seem to apply here.

Robbery (hirâba)

Robbery (*hirâba*) is another *hadd* offence punishable by severe penalties. It is defined as follows:

> Whoever acting alone or in conjunction with others in order to seize property or to commit an offence or for any other reason voluntarily causes or attempts to cause to any person death or hurt or wrongful restraint or fear of instant death or of instant hurt or of instant wrongful restraint in circumstances that renders such person helpless or incapable of defending himself, is said to commit the offence of *hirâba*.[20]

As in classical doctrine, the penalties are imprisonment for life (the modern understanding of banishment) if neither property

---

9. *Zamfara Penal Code, S.229, 231; Bauchi Penal Code, S.227, 229; Kebbi Penal Code, S.228, 230; Jigawa Penal Code, S. 229, 231; Yobe Penal Code, S. 229, 231.*
10. *Kano Penal Code, S. 139, Zamfara Penal Code, S.152. The wording derives not from the Shari'a but from S. 296 of the Penal Code of the Northern Region. The Niger State Penal Code just refers to these sections of robbery in the unamended PC.*

nor a life was taken, amputation of the right hand and left foot if property was taken, and death if a life was taken.[21] The Niger State Penal Code also imposes alternate amputation in cases in which grievous hurt was inflicted during the attack. The Zamfara Penal Code makes a distinction between the case in which only a life has been taken and the case in which both a life and property have been taken. In conformity with the classical doctrine, the penalty in the latter case is crucifixion. Nowhere, however, does the Zamfara Penal Code define this punishment, which is a serious omission since the matter is controversial in classical *Maliki* doctrine. Some *Maliki* authorities held that crucifixion means that the convict's body is exposed on a cross after his having been put to death, whereas others claimed that the convict must first be crucified and then put to death. The Bauchi Penal Code (S. 156 (d)) speaks of "death by impalement (crucifixion)", but does not further define the nature of this punishment.

In classical *Maliki* doctrine, a person who has committed an act constituting robbery will not be punished by the *hadd* penalty if he repents and gives himself up to the authorities before being apprehended. He does remain responsible, however, for any other offence (theft, homicide, grievous hurt) committed during the act. None of the Penal Codes contains such a provision.

Homicide and hurt

The new provisions in regard to homicide and hurt follow essentially (but not entirely) the classical model. The most important element of the classical doctrine is that the kind of punishment depends on the will of the victim's next of kin, or the victim himself in case of hurt. If the homicide was intentional and the victim's next of kin[22] so desire, the perpetrator will be

---

21. Kano Penal Code, S.140; Zamfara Penal Code, S.153; Niger State Penal Code, S.68A (2) (b).
22. The Kano and Zamfara Penal Codes define the next of kin (*waliyy al-dam*) as the male agnatic relatives, which category includes three classes of females: full sister whether alone (ik begrijp dit niet en waar is 'or', dwz 'whether... or...'?], consanguine sister and daughter, who are agnatised by their brothers (S.49). The meaning of the text is unclear, but the last part seems to be in conflict with classical Maliki law, where daughters or sisters may only act as "avengers" in the absence of sons or brothers.

sentenced to suffer retaliation, i.e. death. In case of intentional hurt, the victim determines whether his attacker can be sentenced to retaliation. In classical Shari'a, there was no public prosecutor and the next of kin or the victim would sue the perpetrator. This system has not been adopted. The state prosecutor brings the accused to trial and only at the end, before sentencing, do the next of kin or the victim have the opportunity to give a statement as to whether or not they want the accused to be sentenced to retaliation.

Intentional homicide and retaliation

The crucial question to consider in homicide cases is how intent is defined and established, since that is the first requirement for a sentence of retaliation. Classical *Maliki* doctrine is not very clear about it.[23] In general, intent is assumed if a person attacks another with a weapon or instrument that in general can be considered lethal or if he attacks another in anger and the other person dies. The new Penal Codes are somewhat ambiguous. The Kano Penal Code (S. 142) and the Niger amendment (S. 68A (2)(f)) essentially adopt the definition given in the 1960 Penal Code:

> Whoever being fully responsible *(mukallaf)* causes death (a) by doing an act with the intention of causing death or such hurt as is likely to cause death; or (b) by doing an act with knowledge that he is likely by such act to cause death; or (c) by doing a rash and negligent act, commits the offence of culpable homicide *(qatl al-'amd)*.

---

23 "Homicide according to [the Malikis] is of two kinds: intentional or by error (khata'). Homicide by error occurs when it is caused by an accident or by a person who is legally not capable, or if the perpetrator did not intend [to attack] the victim, or if the victim was killed by an object that usually is not lethal, such as a whip. In such cases there is no retaliation but only the blood price. Intentional homicide is everything else. A pseudo error (shibh khata') is when a person intends to kill someone, but misses [and kills someone else], or if he has killed by means of a whip [or other instrument] which is usually not lethal, or strikes with his fist or with his hand. In these cases there is retaliation. Thus, if the perpetrator beats [someone] with a rod or a whip, which are usually not lethal, or with something heavy like a rock, or has strangled [his victim] or prevented him from eating or drinking until he died, then there is retaliation if the [victim's] death was intended. However, if he only intended to discipline, then he must pay the blood price. ('Abd al-Rahman al-Jaziri, Al-fiqh 'ala al-madhahib al-arba'a. Cairo: n.d., vol. 5, p.256.

The Zamfara Penal Code (S. 199), however, is clearly influenced by classical doctrine. It reads:

> (...) whoever being a *mukallaf* in a state of anger causes the death of a human being (a) with the intention of causing death in [Read: "or". RP] such bodily injury as is probable or likely to cause death with an object either sharp or heavy; or (b) with a light stick or whip or any other thing of that nature which is not intrinsically likely or probable to cause death, commits the offence of intentional homicide (*qatl al-ʿamd*).

This is another example of muddled drafting. The wording implies that the state of anger is a necessary condition for proving intent. This, however, cannot have been meant by the legislator. Interpreting it against the background of classical *Maliki* doctrine, it seems that the "state of anger" as a sign of intent is only relevant with regard to clause (b), since in (a) intent is already indicated by the kind of object used.

The penalty for intentional (or culpable) homicide is death if the next of kin demand it, otherwise it is payment of the blood price (*diya*).[24] Only in the case of treacherous homicide (*qatl ghīla*, defined in S. 50 of both the Zamfara and Kano Penal Codes, as "the act of luring a person to a secluded place and killing him") is the next of kin's position irrelevant, since the perpetrator can be sentenced to death regardless of the demands of the relatives.

The classical *Maliki* law books specify that retaliation is only justified if the victim is of the same or higher value (measured according to the blood price) than the killer, except in the case that the difference is based on gender.[25] If a Muslim kills a Christian or a free person a slave, they cannot be executed for their deeds but will be sentenced to pay the blood price under *Maliki* law. Cases of Muslims killing Christians would fall under the jurisdiction of the Shari'a, the accused being a Muslim. However, none of the Penal Codes has included the provision that retaliation requires that the victim's blood price be equal or

---

24. Kano Penal Code, S. 143; Zamfara Penal Code, S.200; Niger State Code S. 68A (2) (f);
25. This means that a man can be sentenced to death for killing a woman

higher than the killer's. Reportedly, the rule was not applied in colonial times but it is not clear whether the present Shari'a courts will continue this practice.

Blood price (diya)

If the next of kin remit both retaliation and the blood price, the murderer can be sentenced to ten years' imprisonment (Kano Penal Code, S. 143(c)) or, in conformity with classical *Maliki* doctrine, to one hundred lashes with one year imprisonment (Zamfara Penal Code, S. 200). A difficulty inherent in the Kano and Zamfara Penal Codes is that the amount of blood price (*diya*) is not clearly defined. S. 59 in both Penal Codes follows the classical law books and sets its value at 1,000 dinars, 12,000 dirhams or 100 camels. Its value in precious metals according to the classical measures (over 4 KGs of gold, or 36 KGs of silver) is outrageously high, taking into account that before 1960 the value of the blood price varied between £12 and £60 Sterling. In the past, governments in the Islamic world (e.g. the Ottoman Empire, Egypt in the nineteenth century) would fix the value of the blood price in local currency to enhance legal security).

Moreover, it is not clear who determines what amount must be paid if there is a difference in value between the stipulated amounts of gold and silver or the one hundred camels. In classical doctrine, it was the accused who was entitled to make the choice. In this respect Niger State is the only legislating body that has opted for a practical solution: S. 68A (2)(f) sets the amount of *diya* at 4 million Naira (about US$30,000 by the end of 2001).

With regard to the law of *diya* (blood price) there are some glaring contradictions in both the Zamfara and Kano Penal Codes. Any person who has caused the death or injury of another is liable for his victim's blood price (*diya*) regardless of his *mens rea*, i.e. regardless of whether or not he is to blame for it. Even if the killing was accidental, and not the result of any form of negligence, the next of kin are entitled to the blood price. This is acknowledged in the Zamfara and Kano Penal Codes: "Whoever (...) causes the death of any other person by mistake or accident is said to commit unintentional homicide."[26] That

---

26. Kano Penal Code, S.144, Zamfara Penal Code, S.201

mens rea is irrelevant is in accordance with the classical doctrine, since unintentional homicide is regarded as a tort (a civil wrong), giving rise to civil liability. This is a strict liability arising from causation, and not from fault. Hence, the liability of minors and the insane in classical doctrine. However, both the Kano and the Zamfara Penal Codes lay down that *diya* is a punishment.[27] This perspective results in serious contradictions since S. 63 (ii) of both Penal Codes stipulates: "There shall be no criminal responsibility unless an unlawful act or omission is done intentionally or negligently." Homicide by mistake or accident cannot be equated to killing by negligence since the latter offence implies blameworthiness of guilt, which is not a necessary element of the former. Evidence for the tortious character of *diya* for unintentional homicide is that, in classical doctrine, it is not the killer who is liable but his `âqila`, his agnatic relatives. Although the term `âqila` is defined in both the Kano and Zamfara Penal Codes (S. 51), the liability of the `âqila` is not mentioned in the sections on unintentional homicide.

Hurt

The provisions regarding personal injury, or hurt, is also close to classical theory. The voluntarily causing of hurt can be punished by retaliation, i.e. the inflicting of the same grievous hurt on the attacker (e.g. blinding, amputation). At least one sentence of retaliation has been pronounced. On 26 May, 2001 Ahmed Tijani was sentenced in Malunfashi, Katsina, to have his right eye removed after blinding a man in an assault. The victim was given the choice between demanding 'an eye for an eye' and 50 camels.[28] This sentence was pronounced in spite of the fact that Katsina had not yet enacted a Shari'a Penal Code. I have no information on whether the sentence has been carried out.

The victim is entitled to financial compensation if there are no terms for applying retaliation. This could be because the injury is inflicted by mistake or is not serious (i.e. not amounting to "grievous hurt"), because the victim is not equivalent (of the

---

27. See e.g. Zamfara Penal Code, S.202: "Whoever commits the offence of unintentional homicide shall be punished with the payment of *diya*."

28 AFP news summary

same or higher monetary value in terms of *diya*), or because retaliation is impossible since infliction of a similar wound will likely result in death. The compensation, *diya*, is fixed according to a schedule appended to the Code. In addition, the perpetrator is punished by a maximum of 20 lashes and (Zamfara) up to six months' imprisonment.[29] The distinction between hurt and grievous hurt goes back to the Penal Code of 1960 and has no foundation in the Shari'a. The Niger amendment (S. 68A (2)(i)) only vaguely reflects the Shari'a. It does not mention retaliation, and only lays down that in addition to the punishments imposed by the Penal Code of 1960, the convict "shall pay a sum of no less than ₦10,000.00 as compensation to the victim."

Enforcement

A serious problem with regard to the introduction of the new Shari'a Penal Codes is that the police is a federal institution. They are not trained to enforce the locally enacted Penal Codes and, if they are not Muslims, may not be willing to enforce them. This had already led to problems that were aggravated by the fact that in states where alcohol was banned, policemen continued to drink openly and in some cases began to transform their police stations into beer parlours.

Since parts of the population regarded the imposition of an Islamic order as an instrument to eliminate crime, corruption and immorality, the behaviour of the police aroused their anger. As a result of the slackness of the police in enforcing the Shari'a, vigilante groups emerged, calling themselves *hisba* groups.[30] These groups attacked places where prostitutes were said to ply their trade and where alcohol was sold. They took the law into their own hands and excesses occurred on many occasions.

Recognising that these *hisba* groups must be curbed if law and order were to be maintained and also aware of the reluctance of the police in enforcing the Shari'a, some state governments (e.g. Kano), decided to establish their own, government-

---

29. Kano Penal Code, S.163; Zamfara Penal Code, S.216
30 This refers both to the Qur'anic duty of every individual Muslim to "enjoin what is right and forbid what is wrong" (Qur'an 3:104), and the office of *hisba*, or market inspector, who, in classical times would supervise the markets and enforce honest trade.

controlled *hisba* groups. The rules and regulations of the Kano *hisba* committee list mainly religious duties, such as counselling and guiding Muslims who are negligent in their religious duties or do not behave as a good Muslim should. They are not authorised to deal with crime, except in co-operation with the police. In order to make them recognisable to the public, they wear a uniform.

Chapter Three

The Islamic Penal Codes and the Federal Constitution

The question of whether or not the reintroduction of Shari'a criminal law in the Northern states with a Muslim majority is constitutional is hotly debated and highly politicised. The relevant provisions of the 1999 Constitution seem to allow various interpretations. Both the Northern states and the opponents of Islamisation of the legal system of the North contend that there is constitutional support for their positions. It would seem that the Northern states have followed a policy of *faits accomplis*, thus forcing the Federation to choose between reacting to it or silently accepting the situation. So far, the Federation has not taken any measures, although, under serious international pressure, the federal minister of justice sent a letter to the Northern states in February 2002, pointing out that the Shari'a Penal Codes were on many scores unconstitutional. Since the new laws have not yet been challenged judicially,[1] many Northern advocates of the Shari'a codes maintain that the Constitution poses no problem for the introduction of Shari'a criminal law.

If there are conflicts between the new penal codes and the Constitution, there are two ways to resolve them: litigation or negotiation. It is clear that the introduction of these codes have had an adverse effect on the relationship between the North and the South. The positions vis-à-vis each other have hardened, which make it even more difficult to agree on a solution. Let us consider the options.

Possible unconstitutional provisions in the new laws can be challenged in court. S. 1.3 of the Constitution stipulates that if any law is inconsistent with the provisions of the Constitution,

---

1. Attempts to do so by human rights organisations from the South have failed on the ground of lack of *locus standi*

the Constitution shall prevail and the other law shall, to the extent of the inconsistency, be void. Litigation, however, is regarded by many in the North as both an undesirable and an unlikely option. It is undesirable because the issue has become so politicised that any tribunal having to give a judgement in the matter would be forced to make a political decision. This is all the more serious since in the Supreme Court the North is over-represented. Members of the judiciary are concerned that this might affect the credibility of the judicial apparatus.

However, it is for several reasons unlikely that the constitutional issues will be decided by the courts. The first obstacle is the requirement that the constitutionality of the new penal codes can only be challenged in court by a person with *locus standi*, which, in Nigerian law, is interpreted rather strictly. Class actions are not admitted, so that human rights organisations cannot initiate proceedings on this issue. Until recently it has been impossible to find a person who was convicted under these laws and who was willing to appeal his sentence. It seems that this unwillingness is caused both by social pressure to accept the sentence, since opposing it could be seen as criticism of Islam, and by the idea that they deserved the punishment (even amputation) and that their conscience can be at rest. Moreover, it might be a very lengthy process. Some lawyers estimate that it could take at least ten years of litigation in lower courts before the Supreme Court is able to give a final decision.

Negotiation, therefore, would seem to be a better option. This would require the involvement of all states of the Federation. The goal would be a modification of the Constitution on several issues, in which all states would give and take in order, to save in the end, the Federation. I am not in a position to assess the practicality of this solution.

The controversy about the constitutionality of the new penal codes centres on four issues:
- The question of whether states may introduce a religiously-inspired legal system such as the Shari'a;
- The question of the position of the Shari'a within the Nigerian legal system, especially in relation to the constitutional

provision prohibiting the adoption by the Federation or the states of a state religion;

• The possible infringement on the legislative prerogatives of the Federation by states having legislated on issues of evidence in the Shari'a Penal Codes;

• The possible violation of basic human rights guaranteed in the Constitution.

In this chapter, the first three issues will be addressed. The fourth issue will be discussed in the following chapter, taking also into account Nigeria's international human rights commitments.

Shari'a and state religion

Section 10 of the Constitution reads: 'The Government of the Federation or of a State shall not adopt any religion as State religion.' This is generally understood to mean that neither the legislative power nor the executive power may in any way be used to aid, advance, foster, promote or sponsor a religion. Those who are opposed to the extension of the scope of Shari'a justice maintain that the position recently given to it by the Northern states is tantamount to the adoption of Islam as a state religion and, therefore, is in conflict with S. 10 of the Constitution. Many Muslim jurists[2] and politicians, especially those from the North, reject this argument. They argue, correctly as we have seen in Chapter 2, that the Shari'a, including Shari'a penal law, has been an integral part of the Northern legal system up to 1960. In addition, they contend that the introduction of a religiously-inspired law does not amount to the adoption of a state religion, especially since the Shari'a applies only to Muslims and not to Christians. Thirdly, they maintain that the interpretation of S. 10 put forward by the opponents of the re-Islamisation of the legal system of the North is in conflict with those sections of the Constitution (such as S. 275-277, empowering the states to establish Shari'a Courts of Appeal) that accord a special position

---

2. For an eloquent clarification of the Northern position, see Adegbite, A-L. (2000). "Sharia in the context of Nigeria." The Sharia Issue: Working papers for a dialogue. Lagos: 57-82

to the Shari'a. And, finally, they hold that freedom of religion, as guaranteed in S. 38(1) gives Muslims the right to practise their religion, which means to live according to the Shari'a

One could object, however, to this view, and claim that recognition of Muslim civil and personal law is sufficient for Muslims to be able to practise their religion. The introduction of criminal law necessitates an intensive involvement of the state and could be regarded as the adoption of Islam as state religion.

The legislative powers of the states

The second issue I will address is the extent of the legislative powers of state governments vis-à-vis the Federation. Under S. 4 of the 1999 Constitution, the legislative powers in Nigeria are divided between the Federation and the states. Matters mentioned in the Exclusive Legislative List (appended to the Constitution) are exclusively federal matters, while matters mentioned in the Concurrent Legislative List can come under both the legislative power of the Federation and the legislative power of the states. In regard to matters not mentioned in either the Exclusive Legislative List or the Concurrent Legislative List, only the states have the power to legislate. Since penal law is not mentioned in either list, it is evident that this is the domain of state legislation. Indeed, the Penal Code of 1960 was not a federal one, but effective only in the Northern states. However, as appears from the Exclusive Legislative List, there are certain domains related to penal law that are regarded as federal, such as evidence (23), the police (45) and prisons (48). State legislation may not address these topics.

The question to be considered here is not whether states may introduce their own penal laws, but whether or not they may introduce a religiously-inspired law like the Shari'a. There is no controversy about the application of the Shari'a in some fields, such as personal law. In fact, this is recognised by the Constitution (S. 275-277) which authorises the states, if they require, to establish Shari'a Courts of Appeal. These courts have jurisdiction in matters of Islamic personal law. However, the first subsection of S. 277 stipulates that the state may confer on the courts any other jurisdiction. The precise meaning of these words is controversial. The Northern states hold that this clause gives the states the power to extend the jurisdiction of these courts to other domains, whereas others contest this and argue that the wording of the beginning of S. 277(2) ("For the purposes of subsection (1) of this section, the Shari'a Court of Appeal shall be competent to decide..." followed by various aspects of Islamic personal law) restricts the meaning of subsection 1 and forbids the states from conferring other jurisdictions on the Shari'a Courts of Appeal than matters of personal law.

Another argument against the Northern position is S. 244(1). This section lays down that the Federal Court of Appeal is the appellate court for state Shari'a Courts of Appeal. However, appeal to the Federal Court of Appeal from the state Shari'a Courts of Appeal is restricted to matters of Muslim personal law. In many Northern states, however, the Shari'a was applied in other domains than personal law, but qua customary law, and not in its own right. This means that, as in the colonial period, its application is restricted by the repugnancy clause, i.e. it may only be applied if it is not in conflict with written laws or with natural justice, equity and good conscience.

Many Muslim lawyers assert that the Shari'a deserves a proper position in its own right and that the Constitution, by empowering the states to create Shari'a Courts of Appeal, has already recognised the special status of the Shari'a in the Nigerian legal system. When, as from 1999, the Northern states enacted laws to introduce a Shari'a court system to apply the Shari'a, they could maintain that this was in accordance with S. 275(1) of the Constitution.

Conflict with the Legislative Prerogatives of the Federation

A final point where some Shari'a Penal Codes may be in conflict with the Constitution is that the Exclusive Legislative List includes evidence as one of the domains in which only the federal legislature may enact laws. Nevertheless, some Shari'a penal codes contain provisions with regard to evidence: The Kano Penal Code (S. 127, explanation), Kebbi Penal Code (S. 127), and Niger Penal Code (S. 68A (3)(b) stipulate that four male witnesses are required to prove unlawful sexual intercourse. Since the *hadd* offences in particular are subject to strict rules of proof, the constitutional position regarding evidence is an obstacle to the strict application of these rules, for the federal law of evidence admits more forms of legal proof in criminal matters than only confession and the testimony of two (for unlawful intercourse, four) adult Muslim males of good moral reputation. Application of the federal rules would make the enforcement of corporal punishment for these offences much easier.

Chapter Four

The Shari'a Penal Codes and Human Rights

Nigeria's Human Rights Obligations

Chapter IV of the Constitution of 1999 protects most human rights. In addition, Nigeria has committed itself to guarantee basic human rights in various international contexts. The most important is the worldwide context within the framework of the United Nations. In addition, Nigeria has pledged to abide by the human rights standards within the framework of the Organisation of African Unity (the African Charter of Human and Peoples' Rights, ACHPR) and of the Commonwealth. In addition to the Constitution, we will focus on the United Nations conventions and the ACHPR.

After the proclamation of the Universal Declaration of Human Rights in 1948, which, although not binding upon the member states, set the standards for the human rights discourse, the United Nations has successfully formulated a number of international conventions in which human rights are further specified and made binding upon the signatories. Although the sanctions on violations by the States Parties are minimal, these conventions are significant in that they show the commitment of the States Parties. Nigeria has signed all of these conventions. Those relevant to this study are: the International Covenant on Civil and Political Rights 1966, the Convention for the Elimination of All Forms of Discrimination against Women 1979, the Convention against Torture and Other Cruel, Inhuman and Degrading Treatment or Punishment 1984 (henceforth CAT), and the Convention on the Rights of the Child 1989.

The following points represent areas where the Shari'a Penal Codes may be in conflict with human rights:
- Introduction of penalties which can be regarded as torture or cruel, degrading or inhuman punishment;
- Violation of the principle of *nulla poena sine lege*;
- Violation of the principle that all persons are equal before the law;

37

- Limitation of the freedom of religion;
- Violation of the basic rights of children. (CRC Art. 1, 37, 40).

In the discussion we will mostly refer to the Zamfara Penal Code, which can be regarded as the model of most other Shari'a Penal Codes.

Possible conflicts

Torture or cruel, degrading or inhuman punishment

Torture or cruel, degrading or inhuman punishment is outlawed by both the Constitution and the CAT. They lay down that no person shall be subjected to torture or to inhuman or degrading punishments and that states shall take measures to prevent public servants from committing acts of torture or administer such punishment.[1]

Here we have one of the most conspicuous domains of conflict between the new Penal Codes and human rights principles. Few jurists would deny that amputation of limbs and retaliation for grievous hurt such as blinding or the pulling out of teeth are indeed a form of torture. The same is true in regard to death by stoning and crucifixion (at least if the latter punishment is taken to mean that the convict will be killed after having been crucified) and to certain instances of capital punishment in which the perpetrator is put to death in the same way as he killed his victim.[2] If such punishments cannot be regarded as torture, then they certainly constitute cruel, inhuman or degrading punishment. Many Muslim jurists, however, would argue that these qualifications do not apply to the Qur'anic punishments. Since they were imposed by God through the Qur'an, they could never be regarded as unlawful.

It seems highly unlikely that these punishments will be removed from the Northern Penal Codes. As one judge said: "The *hudûd* are a no go area." Instead many jurists try to exercise

---

1. Constitution, S.34; CAT, Art. 1 (1) and 16 (1); ACHPR, Art. 5.
2. Zamfara Penal Code, S.240. In November 2001, a Katsina Shari'a Court sentenced Sani Yakubu Rodi to be stabbed to death in the same way as he had killed his victims. At this moment I do not know whether the sentence has been carried out.

"damage control". They want to make use of the restrictions that under classical Shari'a doctrine make the application of these punishments extremely difficult. In some other Islamic countries where Islamic criminal law has been introduced, such as Pakistan, such mutilating punishments have not been carried out. Their embodiment in the legislation has mainly a symbolic value. According to Northern Nigerian lawyers, similar results could be achieved in Nigeria by a better training of the judges and information campaigns amongst the population.

Nulla poena sine lege
Section 36 (12) of the Constitution stipulates that "a person shall not be convicted of a criminal offence unless that offence is defined and the penalty therefore is prescribed in a written law." This is obviously in conflict with Shari'a criminal law being enforced in Sokoto and Katsina before Shari'a Penal Codes were enacted. In the absence of a written law (although some Muslims jurists would argue that the Shari'a is a written law, since it is found in written books of jurisprudence), the judges were to have recourse to the classical *Maliki* texts. However, even in those states which have enacted Shari'a Penal Codes, the situation is unconstitutional, for all codes (with the exception of the Kano Penal Code) contain a section making punishable any act or omission that is an offence under the Shari'a even if not mentioned in the Penal Code itself.[3] This is also patently repugnant to the principle of S. 36 (12) of the Constitution, as even some Northern Muslim lawyers admit.[4]

Equality before the law
One of the most prominent principles in human rights discourse is that all persons are equal before the law and entitled to the same legal protection. This principle is embodied in S. 42 of the Constitution. The same principle is expressed in international

---

3. Zamfara Penal Code, S.92; Jigawa Penal Code, 92; Bauchi Penal Code, S. 95; Yobe Penal Code, S.92; Kebbi Penal Code, S.93
4. Adegbite, A-L. (2000). "Sharia in the context of Nigeria." The Sharia Issue: Working papers for a dialogue. Lagos:57-82.

human rights instruments.[5] Here we will examine whether the Shari'a Penal Codes violate the principle of equality with regard to gender and religion.

In the new Penal Codes, there are only a few provisions that discriminate on the basis of gender. As in the 1960 Penal Code,[6] the new Penal Codes allow the physical correction of a wife by her husband (Zamfara Penal Code, S. 76 (d)) and stipulate that, because of implied consent, a man is not capable of raping his wife in the sense of the law. The Niger Penal Code, S. 68 (A)(3)(b) is the only one stipulating that in the requirement for proving the offence of *zinâ*, the testimony of men is of greater value than that of women. On the other hand, men are placed in a disadvantageous position in the Kano Penal Code (S. 125), where the punishment for *zinâ* committed by unmarried men is caning as well as imprisonment for one year, whereas unmarried women are only to be punished by caning. On the whole, there is little gender bias in the texts of the new Penal Codes. However, there is a great deal of gender bias in their enforcement. The most prominent form of gender discrimination is the application by Shari'a courts, unwarranted by the Shari'a Penal Codes, of the classical *Maliki* doctrine that extramarital pregnancy constitutes proof of unlawful intercourse.

With regard to religion, it is clear that Muslims and non-Muslims are treated differently. However, I have not found instances of discrimination against non-Muslims, since the Shari'a Penal Codes apply only to Muslims. In fact, this also violates the principle of equality, but then to the advantage of non-Muslims. For example, the punishment for certain forms of theft, amputation for Muslims and imprisonment for Christians, is patently in conflict with this principle. However, since the 1960 Penal Code also distinguished between Muslims and Christians with regard to certain offences (e.g. drinking of

---

5. Art. 14 and 26 ICCPR; "All persons shall be equal before the courts and tribunals." "All persons are equal before the law and are entitled without any discrimination to the equal protection of the law." ACHPR, Art. 3: "Every individual shall be equal before the law; Every individual shall be entitled to equal protection of the law."
6. Section 55 (1) (d), subject to the condition that such correction was lawful under customary law of the spouses.

alcohol), it would seem that such distinctions are accepted and not regarded as an essential violation of the equality principle.

Violations of the freedom of religion

One of the most significant conflicts between the Shari'a and internationally recognised human rights is the Shari'a provision that Muslims cannot change their religion and that, if they do, they face a death sentence. Apostasy (*ridda*) also entails the loss of civil rights, such as the right to be married (the marriage of an apostate is dissolved immediately) and the right to hold property. However, none of the new Penal Codes has included apostasy as a punishable offence, no doubt because the conflict with S. 38 of the Constitution, which explicitly mentions the freedom to change one's religion, was too glaring. This does not necessarily mean that apostasy cannot be punished under these laws. The Zamfara Penal Code, as we have seen, stipulates in S. 92 that acts and omissions that are punishable offences under the Shari'a, may be punished even in the absence of a provision in the Penal Code. It is plausible that those who drafted the law had apostasy in mind.

Since Christians are not governed by the new Shari'a Penal Codes, they cannot be said to suffer from religious oppression. However, the new codes contain some provisions which may affect the practice of traditional religions and magical practices. Section 406 (d) of the Zamfara Penal Code reads:

> Whoever presides at or is present at or takes part in the worship or invocation of any *juju* which has been declared unlawful under the provisions of Section 405 will be punished with death;

The previous Section 405, to which it refers, makes the worship or invocation of *juju* unlawful and explains that "*juju*" includes the worship or invocation of any subject or being other than Allah (S.W.T.). This forms part of Sections 405 to 409 (see Appendix Five), dealing with magical practices and witchcraft. The section in almost identical wording was included in the 1960 Penal Code, but with much lighter punishments. The explanation of S. 405, which extends the meaning of *juju* to the "worship or invocation of any subject or being other than Allah", and the fact that this has been made a capital offence render the provisions dangerous, since they could be used against all religious practices that are deemed un-Islamic. The exact purport of the section is not clear. Since the code only addresses Muslims, the provision seems to refer to persons who regard themselves as Muslims but nevertheless   participate in the practices mentioned in these sections.

Violation of the basic rights of children

In classical Islamic law, maturity begins with puberty. The criterion is a purely physical one: it is established by physical signs such as menstruation and the growth of breasts (women) and the appearance of hair under the armpits and ejaculation (men). This means that children in their early teens can be punished with mutilating *hadd* punishments,[7] and this possibility has already been proven by the sentence on 5 July 2001 of a fifteen year old boy to amputation for theft in Birnin Kebbi, the capital of Kebbi state (see Appendix four).

Both the Zamfara and the Kano Penal Codes, following the 1960 Penal Code, explicitly recognise that parents, guardians, schoolmasters and masters [*wat bedoel je hier, van slaven, of is het dubbel?*] are entitled to physically discipline their children, wards, pupils and servants, as long as such castigation does not amount to grievous hurt and is not unreasonable in kind or degree.[8] This seems to justify quite severe physical injury, since the upper limit (grievous hurt) is defined as emasculation, permanent deprivation of one of the senses, deprivation or destruction of a member or joint, permanent disfigurement of the head and face, fracture or dislocation of a bone or tooth or injuries that endanger life or cause severe bodily pain or render the sufferer unable to pursue his ordinary pursuits (Kano Penal Code, S. 159; Zamfara Penal Code, S. 216).

---

7. Zamfara Penal Code, S.47; 63 (1), 71; Kano Penal Code, S. 47, 62A
8. Zamfara Penal Code, S.76; Kano Penal Code, S.76

Chapter Five

Main Conclusions and Summary

In 2000 and the first half of 2001, eleven Northern states re-Islamised their legal system. Seven of them (Bauchi, Kebbi, Jigawa, Kano, Zamfara, Yobe, Sokoto) introduced Shari'a Penal Codes. One (Niger) amended the existing 1960 Penal Code with provisions of Shari'a criminal law, and four others (Borno, Gombe, Kaduna, Katsina) are expected to enact Shari'a Penal Codes in the near future. These Penal Codes have adopted most of the provisions of the 1960 Penal Code, and added new provisions on the Qur'anic offences (*hudûd* offences):

- Theft
- Unlawful sexual intercourse
- Robbery
- Defamation
- Drinking of alcohol

The Islamic law of homicide and hurt had also been added (with as punishment retaliation (*qisâs*) or monetary compensation (*diya*)).

- Except in the states of Zamfara and Niger, where the government took the initiative, the Shari'a Penal Codes were enacted against the wish of the authorities under strong popular pressure.

- The recently enacted Shari'a Penal Codes violate basic human rights on several scores. The most important area of conflict is that these laws prescribe for certain offences penalties which must be regarded as torture or degrading and inhuman punishment.

- The introduction of Islamic criminal law is a state act with a highly symbolic value, as it becomes clear from other countries where Islamic criminal law has been adopted. It is also an irreversible process. For a political leader to advocate its abolition would be political suicide. Lawyers in the North are well aware of this. As a Northern High Court judge explained: "The law of *hudûd* is a no go area." What can be done, however, is "damage control". Outside pressure to annul the Shari'a Penal Codes will be ineffective and can only lead to antagonism and a defensive attitude.

- The introduction of Islamic criminal law does not necessarily mean that the harsh, mutilating punishments it prescribes are actually applied. In some countries with Islamic criminal law, such penalties are not enforced. This is, for instance, the case in Libya and Pakistan, where Islamic criminal law was introduced by legislation in 1973 and 1979 respectively. In other countries, such as Sudan, these punishments were applied only during the first period after the introduction. It is possible that Northern Nigeria will follow the same path, after the initial fervour has passed away. Within the framework of Islamic law, there are sufficient legal possibilities to restrict and even preclude the imposition of these penalties, e.g. by demanding very strict standards of evidence and by allowing many defence pleas based on uncertainty. There are many such defences listed in classical doctrine. Thus, for instance, a creditor cannot be sentenced to amputation for having stolen money from a debtor in arrears, when his defence is that he believed the money was owed him. This will require a more thorough training of the police and the Shari'a judges as well as enlightenment campaigns among the population. It is important that such projects and campaigns be conducted by local organisations.

- The introduction of Shari'a Penal Codes may in some areas be in conflict with the federal constitution. They infringe on federal legislative prerogatives (e.g. in the field of evidence) and contradict the principle that offences and their punishments must be founded on written law (most of the Shari'a Penal Codes contain provisions that acts and omissions that are punishable under the Shari'a, may be punished by the Shari'a courts, even if the Penal Code does not mention them). Finally, it is a moot point whether the introduction of Shari'a codes is a violation of section 10 of the Constitution, which prohibits the adoption by the Federation or the states of a state religion.

- The first Shari'a Penal Codes enacted in Zamfara shows every sign of hasty drafting: incorrect cross-references, incorrect and defective wording, omissions, and contradictions. In spite of these defects, five other states have adopted the Zamfara code verbatim or with minor changes. The Kano Penal Code, which is slightly different, has similar defects. These imperfections in the legislation are in the first place a result of the time pressure under which the preparatory committees were forced to work. There was an urgent political need for the introduction of a Shari'a Penal Code, either from above (Zamfara and Niger) or from below (the other states). A factor that also contributed to the sloppy drafting of the codes was a general awareness that these codes were only of secondary importance and no more than instruments to implement the Shari'a to which the courts could have recourse in case of silence or ambiguity of the enacted law.

- In September 2001, the Institute of Islamic Legal Studies at the Ahmadu Bello University (Zaria) with federal backing, initiated a project to prepare a unified Shari'a Penal Code for the North. Its immediate aim is to create a larger jurisdiction of the Shari'a Penal Code, which will enhance legal certainty and facilitate the training of judicial staff and police personnel. Moreover, it aims at redressing the poor drafting. Among those involved in the project are jurists who would like to emphasise the restrictions and limitations that would make the application of the severe Qur'anic punishments more difficult. At the moment it is difficult to say how much weight their views carry, but it is clear that they deserve support.

- The Shari'a Penal Codes were introduced with little to no preparation. This means that the judiciary was not trained to work with these codes. Moreover, there is a problem in enforcing them since the police is a federal institution and policemen are not trained, and are often not willing, to enforce these codes completely.

- The lax attitude of the police combined with the religious fervour of the population have led to the emergence of Islamic vigilante groups known as *hisba* groups. In many instances these have begun to take the law into their own hands, which has often resulted in violence and disorder. The government is now trying to control the situation by establishing its own *hisba* groups, and instructing them to co-operate with the police.

One cannot emphasise enough that the local population is often ignorant of the exact provisions of the Shari'a and of their rights if they are tried before a Shari'a court. It is desirable that information campaigns be conducted through local organisations.

APPENDICES

Appendix One

Term of Reference

Study on the Introduction of Criminal Shari'a Law in Northern Nigeria

The consultant will:

Briefly describe the role of Shari'a in the legal system(s) of Northern Nigeria until the present, in order to sketch the background against which the recent introduction of Shari'a as the source of criminal law must be analysed;

Describe and analyse how Shari'a criminal law was introduced, what legislation has been enacted with respect to substantive rules, the judiciary and rules of procedure, and how this has affected the penal system that was effective before the introduction of Shari'a criminal law;

Analyse the different methods used by the Northern states in introducing Shari'a criminal law as well as the differences between the Islamic penal codes enacted by these states and examine their conformity or departure from the rules of classical Shari'a law;

Describe and analyse how Shari'a criminal law has been applied so far and give an overview of verdicts according to Shari'a criminal law and their execution;

Briefly describe the controversy regarding the constitutionality of the introduction of Shari'a criminal law and analyse and contrast the positions and arguments of the parties in the controversy;

Analyse how Shari'a criminal law as introduced in Northern Nigeria relates to internationally accepted human rights norms and standards.

The regional scope of the study will be dependent upon the availability at the instance of the EU coordinator of civil society and human rights, the relevant legal texts before the commencement of the consultancy.

Appendix Two

Programme of the mission

Wednesday September 12th (Lagos)
Prof. (Mrs) Jadesola Akande
Women, Law & Development Centre Nigeria (WLDCN)

Thursday September 13th (Lagos)
Dr. (Mrs) Ayesha Imam, BAOBAB
Mr. Tunde Fagbohunle, solicitor, Aluko & Oyebode Law Firm

Saturday September 15th (Kano)
Prof. Yadudu, Professor Faculty of Law, Bayero University, Kano
Dr. (Mrs) Zainab Kabir, Dept. of Political Science, Bayero
University, Kano.
Hon. Attorney General of Kano State, Alhaji Balarabe Bello Rogo,
Ministry of Justice, Kano.
Mr Abubakar B. Mahmud (SAN) & Justice Patricia Mahmud

Sunday September 16th (Kano)
Prof. Sani Zahraddin
Former Vice Chancellor Bayero University, Kano and now Pro-
Chancellor and Chairman of Council, University of Benin.
Mr. Mallam Muzzamil Sani Hanga
Legal Practitioner and Secretary of the Drafting Committee of
the Kano Shari'a Penal Code
Mr. Alhaji Kuliya Alkali, Chief Imam of Kano and former Grand
Kadi of Kano State.

Monday September 17th (Kano)
Dr. Aminuddin Abubakar, Chairman *Hisba* Committee, Kano
Faculty of Law, Bayero University Kano, guest lecture 'From
Jurist's Law to Statute Law: What Happens When Shari'a is

Codified?' by Prof. Peters.
Faculty of Law, Bayero University, Kano
Chief Judge of Kano State Mr. Sanusi Chiroma Yusuf
Tuesday September 18th (Zaria)

Institute of Islamic Legal Studies, Ahmadu Bello University, Zaria: Guest lecture 'From Jurist's Law to Statute Law: What Happens When Shari'a is Codified?' by Prof. Peters
Centre for Islamic Legal Studies, Ahmadu Bello University Zaria.
Dr. I.N. Sada, Director of Centre for Islamic Legal Studies, Ahmadu Bello University, Zaria.
Prof. Kumo, Head of the Institute for Administrative Law, Ahmadu Bello University, Zaria.

Appendix Three

Laws and Law Codes used for this study

BAUCHI STATE

Shari'a Penal Code, 2001

Shari'a Courts (Administration of Justice and Certain Consequential Changes) Law, 2001

GOMBE

A bill on Shari'a Penal Code is before their House of Assembly. The text could not be consulted.

JIGAWA

Law 7/2000: A law to Establish Shari'a Courts in Jigawa State

Shari'a Penal Code, 2000

KADUNA STATE

Area Courts (Repeal) Law 2001 (Law 6/2000) [effective from 2 November 2001]

Shari'a Courts Law, 2001 (law 7/2000) [effective from 2 May 2001]

KANO

Kano State Shari'a Penal Code. Law 2000

Criminal Procedure Code (Amendment) Law 2000 [effective from 1 Ramadan 1421]

Kano State Shari'a Courts Law 2000 [effective from 1 Ramadan 1421]

KATSINA

Katsina State Shari'a Commission Law (Law 3 / 2000) [effective from 20 April 2000]

Shari'a Courts Law 2000 (Law 5 / 2000) [effective 1 Aug. 2000]

Islamic Penal System (Adoption) Law 2000 (Law 6 / 2000)

Reportedly, a bill on Shari'a Penal Code was passed by the House of Assembly is with the Governor for his assent. The text could not be consulted.

KEBBI STATE

Penal Code (Amendment) Law 2000 (Law 21 / 2000), amending

Penal Code Law of 1960 [effective from 1 Dec. 2000]

Kebbi State Shari'a (Administration of Justice) Law, 2000 (Law 3 / 2000) [effective from 1 Dec. 2000]

NIGER STATE

Criminal law

Law to amend the Penal Code Law Cap 94. HB. 4/2000, enforced 4-5 2000

This is a law to amend the Niger Penal Code in order to introduce offences and penalties in line with the Shari'a

Law to amend the Criminal Procedure Law Cap 35. HB. 5/ 2000

Amendment to the Criminal procedure Code to adapt it to the changes in the Penal Code.

Laws regarding Shari'a courts

Law to make provisions for the amendment of Shari'a Court of Appeal Law cap. 122 in order to review the jurisdiction of Shari'a Court of Appeal and for connected purposes. Enforced 4-5 2000 (NSLN 6/2000; HB 2/2000)

Law to amend the Area Courts Law Cap 8. HB. 6/2000 (enforced 4-5 2000)

Law to amend the Districts Courts Law (NSNL 5; HB. 1/2000)

Laws amending liquor licensing regulations, enforced 4-5 2000 NSLN 4/2000 and HB.7/2000

SOKOTO

Shari'a Criminal Procedure Code Law, 2000.

Shari'a Courts Law, 2000 (Law 2 / 2000)

Shari'a Penal Code Law, 2000 [effective from 31 January 2001]

YOBE STATE

Shari'a Penal Code, 2001 [effective from 25 April 2001]

ZAMFARA

Zamfara State Shari'a penal code. [effective from 27-1 2000]

Shari'a Criminal Procedure Code Law (Law 18 / 2000)

Shari'a Courts Establishment Law, 1999 (Law 5 / 1999)

Shari'a Court of Appeal Law Cap 13 Amendment Law, 2000 (Law 6 / 2000) [effective 27-1 2000]

Area Courts Repeal Law, 2000 (Law 13 / 2000) [effective 27-1 2000]

Survey of events connected with and sentences pronounced under Shari'a criminal law

This survey is based on press summaries of AFP

Bauchi-State

28-02-2001 Bauchi is the 10th State to adopt the Shari'a.

01-06-2001: Shari'a came into force, with 63 appointed shari'a court judges.

22-06-2001 Several mosques were destroyed during riots which started after a dispute over bus seat arrangements. Apparently, a bus driver asked Christian passengers not to mix.

04-07-2001: Many dozens of people were killed and thousands were forced to flee in ethnic and religious clashes. Christian minorities feel threatened by Shari'a.

Borno-State

10-01-2001 In Maiduguri, Muslim youths have burned down churches and beer parlours after witnessing the first eclipse of the third Millennium.

03-06-2001 Christians in Borno said they will disobey Shari'a, which took effect as from 01-06-2001.

Gombe-State

22-05-2001 25 people injured and a church and other buildings burnt down during riots between Christians and Muslims. The riots started when three Christian youths came out of a church with a placard saying 'no Shari'a'.

Jigawa-State

02-08-2000: Announcement of introduction of Shari'a later this year.

22-06-2001 In Gwaram, Jigawa-State, five churches were burnt down during riots over a book written by a Christian and considered blasphemy by Muslims.

9-5-2002: An Islamic Shari'a court in Dutse, has sentenced a 50 year old man to death by stoning for raping an underage girl. He reportedly confessed in court and is also to receive 100 strokes of the cane and pay compensation of about 75 U.S. dollars to the victim.

Kaduna-State

02-2000: Religious riots claim some thousand lives.

02-2000: Kaduna officials point out: the Shari'a is not to be enforced in Christian areas.

05-2000: Another 300 people died during riots and many properties destroyed.

28-03-2001: Police banned a planned seminar on Islamic law by the Civil Rights Congress, who wanted to discuss the legality of Sharia. The Police referred to the riots.

03-05-2001: The Governor of Kaduna passes a Bill which will implement Islamic courts in Kaduna.

27-08-2001: Former military leader Muhammadu Buhari calls for introduction of Shari'a throughout Nigeria.

Kano-State

04-2000 Banning of gambling, prostitution and alcohol.

18-06-2000 Denial by the government of the fleeing of Christians because of the introduction of Shari'a.

06-2000 Introduction of Shari'a.

08-2000 Demonstrations against Bill Clinton in Kano: he would object to the implementation of Shari'a in parts of the country.

26-11-2000 Sharia came into force.

22-12-2000 Kano-State prohibits drinking of alcohol at police stations, *burukutu* included. This goes for the Christian policemen as well as the Muslim policemen.

24-12-2000 200 women have been arrested after being seen talking to men in Kano. They are questioned about prostitution and adultery. The arrests came after a complaint from the Government's Adviser on Religious Affairs.

02-01-2001 Christian trader claims to have been flogged by *Hisbah*, a group which monitors the strict application of shari'a.

03-01-2001 Nugu Abdullahi and Sa'adu Aminu were given 80 lashes each for drinking alcohol. The crowds shouted '*Allahu Akbar*' during the first sharia-sentence in Kano-State.

08-01-2001 Islamic clergy urged Muslims to boycott an AIDS-seminar because of conflict with Sharia. AIDS-seminars would increase promiscuity.

25-02-2001 The 'assistants' of the police in Kano, the *Hisbah*, attack a truck driver and his truck, which is carrying beer, and a press centre which includes a bar.

17-04-2001 Deputy Governor of Kano leads raids on hotels to crack down on prostitution, in line with Sharia.

17-05-2001 Five Anglicans are accused of abducting 2 Christian girls who were to be married off by their father who has been a Muslim for four years.

22-06-2001 The Government of Kano-State banned women from participating in sporting events and state dance troupe.

21-08-2001 Hotel and bar owners in Kano-City threaten to take self-defence measures if the violence and vandalism do not stop. These acts are mostly committed by *Hisbah*-members.

23-08-2001 Kano-based human rights group *Network for Justice* went to the High Court to challenge the detention of Yakubu Musa, leader of the hardline *Izala* Muslim sect an advocate of Shari'a in Nigeria.

Katsina-State

01-08-2000: Introduction and coming into force of Shari'a.

08-2000: Two men, found guilty of stealing a table fan, were given 20 lashes.

16-11-2000: Lawal Sada found guilty of fornication and sentenced to 1-year imprisonment and a 100 lashes in the town of Malunfashi.

22-12-2000: Katsina-State wants to ban the mixing of men and women in public. Only relatives can mix outside and in public buildings.

11-01-2001: Attine Tanko, girlfriend of Lawal Sada, was found guilty on 15-11-2000 and awaits her punishment of a 100 lashes after she has given birth to her baby.

09-03-2001 Teacher Umaru Bubeh is sentenced to 80 lashes for drinking alcohol and drinks some more whiskey in front of the judge, challenging him.

26-05-2001 In Malunfashi, Ahmed Tijani is sentenced to have his right eye removed after blinding a man in an assault. The victim could choose between 'an eye for an eye' and 50 camels.

29-08-2001 Judges in Katsina challenge in court a plan by the state government to screen the 65 Islamic court judges. It would be unconstitutional.

18-08-2002: Amina Lawal sentenced by the Upper Shari'a Court of Funtua to be stoned to death for unlawful sexual intercourse proven by her extramarital pregnancy. The court upheld the sentence issued on 22-3 by the Bakori Shari'a Court.

Kebbi-State

21-07-2000 Kebbi State House passes Shari'a unanimously in capital Birnin Kebbi.

01-12-2000 Shari'a came into force.

08-12-2000 Emir of Gwandu has been charged with marrying off a young girl twice, which is an offence under Shari'a: a woman can only have one husband.

03-01-2001 Kebbi-State threatens women to dress decently, *'hijab'*-wise, or face the wrath of the (Islamic) law.

25-07-2001 A 15-year-old boy is convicted to have his hand amputated for theft in the state capital Birnin Kebbi. He allegedly stole 32,000 naira (approximately US$ 285). No date has been announced for the execution of sentence.

09-2001 A male who was found guilty of abusing a 7-year-old boy is sentenced to stoning to death (*rajm*).

Niger-State

Early 2000 Introduction of sharia.

Sokoto-State

Early 2000 Introduction of Shari'a.

02-08-2000 Shari'a came into force.

18-06-2001 A man and a woman, Hussaini Mamman Zangalawa and Hauwa'u Garba Kalambaina, could face death by stoning (*rajm*) if found guilty in the 1st adultery case since the introduction of shari'a in Northern Nigeria. The judge ordered a mental examination.

07-07-2001 After stealing a goat and ₦6,000, Umanu Aliyu has been punished by the removal of his right hand: it was the third hand-amputation in Northern Nigeria since the introduction of shari'a.

13-07-2001 Lawali Garba is sentenced to amputation of his hand after being found guilty of stealing car parts, worth $152 dollars. He has 30 days to appeal the decision.

15-08-2001 2 officials were given 40 lashes after stealing $1.500 dollars they were supposed to give to a retired official.

9-10-2001, Safiya Hussaini Tungar-Tudu was sentenced to death by stoning by the Upper Sharia Court in Gwadabawa, Sokoto State, for *zinâ* proven by her extramarital pregnancy. On 25 March 2002, she was acquitted in appeal.

23-01-2002: 28 Year old Hafsatu Abubakar acquitted of charges of *zinâ* based on extramarital pregnancy. She had withdrawn her earlier confession and statement that she had never been married and declared that she had been married before but was divorced two years previously and that her former husband was the child's father. The Court acquitted her on the ground of the conflicting testimonies about the date of the divorce, regarded the former husband as the child's father but did not want to force him to name the child after himself.

Yobe-State

08-08-2000 Introduction of shari'a.

01-10-2000 Coming into force of shari'a.

Zamfara-State

October 1999 Introduction of shari'a.

27-01-2000 shari'a came into force.

24-03-2000 Amputation of hand in capital Gusau inflicted on Bello Garki Zangebi for stealing cattle.

19-07-2000 State Legislator Alhaji Haruna Kalele denies competence of Shari'a court in his case in which he has been accused of forgery and perjury.

09-2000 Pregnant 17-year old girl, Bariya Ibrahim Magazu, found guilty of pre-marital sex was sentenced to 180 lashes, due *27-01-2001*, at least 40 days after she had had her baby.

23-09-2000 For stealing three bicycles, Musa Gummi is sentenced to have his limb amputated.

23-09-2000 A public flogging in Gusau for Lawali Jekada Kaura Namoda (80 lashes) and Karibu Salisu (50 lashes and 6 months imprisonment) for drinking and stealing a 3$-shirt. Offence, arrest, conviction and punishment occurred on the same day.

17-04-2001 A male is sentenced to 80 lashes for falsely accusing his neighbour of sodomy (*qadhf*).

05-05-2001 Authorities have amputated the hand of Lawali Inchitara; he was found guilty of theft of eight bicycles.

12-08-2001 In Gusau, 20-year-old Amina Abdullahi, is sentenced to 100 lashes for illicit intercourse with unmarried man.

01-09-2001 Zamfara Governor Ahmed Sani said his government introduced Shari'a 'purely on religious grounds' while others did so for political reasons.

Relevant provisions of the Shari'a Penal Codes

In this appendix most sections are listed that contain the provisions of Islamic criminal law, as well as those that are referred to in the text of the report. Point of departure has been the Zamfara Penal Code. In those instances where the Kano Penal Code deviates from the text of the Zamfara Penal Code, this has been indicated.

General offences and punishments
Any act or omission which is not specifically mentioned in this Shari'a Penal Code but is otherwise declared to be an offence under the *Qur'an*, *Sunnah* and *Ijtihad* of the *Maliki* School of Islamic thought shall be an offence under this code and such act or omission shall be punishable:

(a) With imprisonment for a term which may extend to 5 years, or
(b) With caning which may extend to 50 lashes, or
(c) With fine which may extend to ₦5,000.00 or with any two of the above punishments.

NB The Kano penal code lacks this section as it was considered unconstitutional (S. 36.12 Constitution – nulla poena sine lege).

Punishments
1. The punishments to which offenders are liable under the provisions of this Shari'a Penal Code are:

(a) death (*qatl*);
(b) forfeiture and destruction of property (*al-musadarah wal ibadah*);

(c)   imprisonment (*sijn*);
(d)   detention in a reformatory (*habs fie islahiyyat*);
(e)   fine (*gharamah*);
(f)   caning (*jald*);
(g)   amputation (*qat'*);
(h)   retaliation (*qisas*);
(i)   blood-wit (*diyyah*);
(j)   restitution (*radd*);
(k)   reprimand (*tawbikh*);
(l)   public disclosure (*tash-heer*);
(m) boycott (*hajar*);
(n)   exhortation (*wa'az*);
(o)   compensation (*arsh, hukumah*);
(p)   closure of premises;
(q)   warning.

2   Nothing in this section shall prevent a court dealing with an offender in accordance with the Probation of Offender Law.

NB The Kano penal code lists its possible punishments in S. 92

Zina defined
Whoever, being a man or a woman fully responsible, has sexual intercourse through the genital of a person over whom he has no sexual rights and in circumstances in which no doubt exists as to the illegality of the act, is guilty of the offence of *zina*.

Punishment for Zina
Whoever commits the offence of *zina* shall be punished:

(a)   with caning of one hundred lashes if unmarried, and shall also be liable to imprisonment for a term of one year; or
(b)   if married, with stoning to death (*rajm*).

EXPLANATION: Mere penetration is sufficient to constitute the sexual intercourse necessary to the offence of *zina*.
NB S. 125 – punishment for zina - of the Kano Penal Code states:

Whoever commits the offence of zina shall be punished:
with caning of a 100 lashes if he is yet to marry, and shall also be liable to imprisonment for the term of one year; or in the case of male; (...)[sic]
This Kano Section stipulates that males, additional to the Zamfara Penal Code, face 1 year imprisonment, if unmarried.

Rape defined

1 A man is said to commit rape who, save in the case referred in subsection (b), has sexual intercourse with a woman in any of the following, circumstances:

(i) against her will;
(ii) without her consent,
(iii) with her consent, when her consent has been obtained by putting her in fear of death or of hurt;
(iv) with her consent, when the man knows that he is not her husband and that her consent is given because she believes that he is another man to whom she is or believes herself to be lawfully married;
(v) with or without her consent, when she is under fifteen years of age or of unsound mind.

2 Sexual intercourse by a man with his own wife is not rape.

EXPLANATION: Mere penetration is sufficient to constitute the sexual intercourse necessary to the offence of rape.

Punishment for Rape
Whoever commits rape, shall be punished:

(a) with caning of one hundred lashes if unmarried, and shall also be liable to imprisonment for a term of one year; or
(b) if married with stoning to death *(rajm)*
(c) in addition to either (a) or (b) above shall also pay the dowry of her equals *(sadaq al-mithli)*.

NB The Kano Penal Code extends the punishment for rape if unmarried to life imprisonment (S. 127).

Additionally, S. 127 of the Kano Penal Code lays down that *zina* can only be proven by 4 or 8 witnesses or confessions. The Zamfara Penal Code is silent in this respect.

Sodomy defined
Whoever has carnal intercourse against the order of nature with any man or woman is said to commit the offence of sodomy: Provided that whoever is compelled by the use of force or threats or without his consent to commit the act of sodomy upon the person of another or be the subject of the act of sodomy, shall not be deemed to have committed the offence.

Punishment for Sodomy
Whoever commits the offence of sodomy shall be punished:

(a) with caning of one hundred lashes if unmarried, and shall also be liable to imprisonment for the term of one year; or
(b) if married with stoning to death (*rajm*).

EXPLANATION: Mere penetration is sufficient to constitute carnal intercourse necessary to the offence of sodomy.

Incest defined

(1)   Whoever, being a man, has sexual intercourse with a woman who is and whom he knows or has reason to believe to be his daughter, his grand-daughter, his mother or any other of his female ascendant or descendants, his sister or the daughter of his sister or brother or his paternal or maternal aunt has committed the offence of incest.

(2)   Whoever, being a woman, voluntarily permits a man who is and whom she knows or has reason to believe to be her son, her grandson, her father or any other of her male ascendants or descendants, her brother or the son of her brother or sister or her paternal or maternal uncle to have sexual intercourse with her, has committed the offence of incest.

Punishment for Incest
Whoever commits incest shall be punished:

(a) with caning of one hundred lashes if unmarried, and shall also be liable to imprisonment for a term of one year; or
(b) if married with stoning to death (*rajm*).

Lesbianism defined
Whoever being a woman engages another woman in carnal intercourse through her sexual organ or by means of stimulation or sexual excitement of one another has committed the offence of Lesbianism.

Punishment for Lesbianism
Whoever commits the offence of lesbianism shall be punished with caning which may extend to fifty lashes and in addition be sentenced to a term of imprisonment which may extend to six months.

EXPLANATION: The offence is committed by the unnatural fusion of the female sexual organs and or by the use of natural or artificial means to stimulate or attain sexual satisfaction or excitement.

Bestiality defined
Whoever being a man or woman has carnal intercourse with any animal is said to commit the offence of bestiality.

Punishment for Bestiality
Whoever commits the offence of bestiality shall be punished with caning of fifty lashes and in addition shall be sentenced to a term of imprisonment of six months.

EXPLANATION: Mere penetration is sufficient to constitute the carnal intercourse necessary to the offence of bestiality.

Qadhf defined
Whoever by words either spoken or reproduced by mechanical

means or intended to be read or by signs or by visible representations makes or publishes any false imputation of *zina* or sodomy concerning a chaste person (muhsin), or contests the paternity of such person even where such person is dead, is said to commit the offence of *qadhf*.

Provided that a person is deemed to be chaste *(mühsin)* who has not been convicted of the offence of *zina* or sodomy.

Punishment for Qadhf

Whoever commits the offence of qadhf shall be punished with eighty lashes of the cane; and his testimony shall not be accepted thereafter unless he repents before the court.

Remittance for the offence of Qadhf

The offence of *qadhf* shall be remitted in any of the following cases:

(a)   where the complainant (*maqzuf*) pardons the accuser (*qazif*)
(b)   where a husband accuses his wife of zina and undertakes the process of mutual imprecation (*lian*).
(c)   where the complainant (maqzuf) is a descendant of the accuser (*qazif*).

Theft defined

The offence of theft shall be deemed to have been committed by a person who covertly, dishonestly and without consent, takes any lawful and movable property belonging to another, out of its place of custody (*hirz*) and valued not less than the minimum stipulated value (nisab) without any justification.

Punishment for theft

Whoever commits the offence of theft punishable with *hadd* shall be punished with amputation of the right hand from the joint of the wrist; and where the offender is convicted for the second theft shall be punished with the amputation of the left foot; and where the offender is convicted for the third theft shall be punished with the amputation of the left hand from the joint of the wrist, and where the offender is convicted for the fourth theft shall be punished with the amputation of the right foot; and where the offender is convicted for the fifth or subsequent thefts, he shall be imprisoned for a term not exceeding one year.

Theft not punishable with *Hadd* defined
Whoever commits the offence of theft that does not meet the requirement of hirz *or nisab* as provided under section 144 is said to commit the offence of theft not punishable with *hadd*.

Remittance of the *Hadd* for theft
The penalty of *hadd* for theft shall be remitted in any of the following cases:

(a)   Where the offence was committed by ascendant against descendant;

(b)   Where the offence was committed between spouses within their matrimonial home; provided the stolen property was not under the victim's lock and key;

(c)   Where the offence was committed under circumstances of necessity and the offender did not take more than he ordinarily requires to satisfy his need or the need of his dependants;

(d)   Where the offender believes in good faith that he has a share (or a right or interest) in the said stolen property and the said stolen property does not exceed the share (or the right or interest to the equivalent of the minimum value of the property *(nisab)*;

(e)   Where the offender retracts his confession before execution of the penalty in cases where proof of guilt was based only on the confession of the offender;

(f)   Where the offender returns or restitutes the stolen property to the victim of the offence and repents before he was brought to trial, he being a first time offender;

(g)   Where the offender was permitted access to the place of custody *(hirz)* of the stolen property;

(h) Where the victim of the offence is indebted to the offender and is unwilling to pay, and the debt was due to be discharged prior to the offence, and the value of the property stolen is equal to, or does not exceed the debt due to the offender to the extent of the *nisab*.

Punishment for theft not punishable by *Hadd*

Whoever commits the offence of theft under section 146 or where the punishment of theft was remitted under section 147 shall be punished with imprisonment for a term which may extend to one year and shall also be liable to caning which may extend to fifty lashes.

NB The Kano Penal Code has included S. 134B – punishment for theft of Government money and property or bank and company:

Whoever is a public servant or a staff of a private sector including bank or company connives with somebody or some other people or himself and stole public funds or property under his care or somebody under his jurisdiction, he shall be punished with amputation of his right hand wrist (...).

Punishment for drinking alcohol

Whoever drinks alcohol or any intoxicant voluntarily, shall be punished with caning of eighty lashes.

Punishment for dealing in alcoholic drinks

Whoever prepares alcohol by either manufacturing, pressing, extracting or tapping whether for himself or for another; or transports, carries or loads alcohol whether for himself or for another; or trades in alcohol by buying or selling or supplying premises by either storing or leasing out premises for the storing or preserving or consumption or otherwise dealing or handling in any way alcoholic drinks shall be punished with caning which may extend to forty lashes or with imprisonment for a term which may extend to six months or with both.

Punishment for drunkenness in a public or private place
Whoever is found drunk or drinking in a public or private place; and conducts himself in a disorderly manner, to the annoyance of any person; incapable of taking care of himself, shall in addition to the punishments specified in section 149 above, be punished with imprisonment for a term which may extend to six months or with a fine which may extend to two thousand naira or with both.

NB The Kano Penal Code adds S. 136.2:

> Whoever takes or injects or inhales any substance for the purpose of intoxication shall be punished with caning which may extend to 80 lashes or with imprisonment which may extend to one year or both.

Hirabah defined
Whoever acting alone or in conjunction with others in order to seize property or to commit an offence, or for any other reasons voluntarily causes or attempts to cause to any person death or hurt or wrongful restraint or fear of instant death or of instant hurt, or of instant wrongful restraint in circumstances that renders such person helpless or incapable of defending himself, is said to commit the offence *of hirabah*.

The Bauchi Penal Code (S. 155) has a different definition:
Hirabah (Brigandage and Armed Robbery) occurs when a person acting singly or in concert with others, commits theft through violence or profits from the fact that his victim(s) are far from help and openly seizes them or their goods, through:
    a. the use of narcotics;
    b. enticement and ambush;
    c. the use of naked violence including murder in any area.

Punishment for *Hirabah*
Whoever commits *hirabah* shall be punished:
(a) With imprisonment for life where the offence was committed without seizure of property or causing death.

(b) With amputation of the right hand from the wrist and the left foot from the ankle where property was seized, but death was not caused.

(c) With death sentence where death was caused, but property was not seized.

(d) With crucifixion, where murder was committed and property was seized. (In the Bauchi Penal Code this subsection reads: "with death by impalement (crucifixion) where death was caused and property seized.")

Making preparation to commit *Hirabah*

Whoever makes any preparation for committing the offence of *hirabah*, shall be punished with imprisonment for a term not exceeding one year and shall also be liable to caning which may extend to fifty lashes.

Belonging to gang of persons associated for the purpose of committing *Hirabah*

Whoever belongs to a gang of persons associated for the purpose of committing *hirabah*, shall be punished with imprisonment for a term which may extend to one year and shall also be liable to caning which may extend to fifty lashes.

Intentional homicide defined

Except in the circumstances mentioned in section 204, whoever being a *mukallaf* in a state of anger causes the death of a human being;

(a) with the intention of causing death in such bodily injury as is probable or likely to cause death with an object either sharp or heavy; or

(b) with a light stick or whip or any other thing of that nature which is not intrinsically likely or probable to cause death, commits the offence of intentional homicide *(qatl al-amd)*.

NB: The Kano Penal Code has adopted the definition given in the 1960 Penal Code in S. 142 – intentional homicide defined: Whoever being fully responsible *(mukallaf)* causes death (a) by doing an act with the intention of causing death or such hurt as is likely to cause death; or (b) by doing an act with knowledge that he is likely by such act to cause death; or (c) by doing a rash and negligent act, commits the offence of culpable homicide (*qatl al amd*).

Punishment for intentional homicide

Whoever commits the offence of intentional homicide shall be punished:-

(a)   with death; or

(b)   where the relatives of the victim remit the punishment in (a) above, with the payment of *diya; or*

(c)   where the relatives of the victim remit the punishment in (a) and (b) above, with caning of one hundred lashes and with imprisonment for a term of one year: Provided that in cases of intentional homicide by way of *gheelah* or *hirabah*, the punishment shall be with death only.

NB The Kano Penal Code: in S. 143.c the punishment (mentioned in the similar Zamfara S. 200.c) is not one hundred lashes plus imprisonment for a term of one year (see above), but imprisonment for a period of ten years.

Unintentional homicide defined

Whoever being a *mukallaf* causes the death of any other person by mistake or accident, is said to commit unintentional homicide.

Punishment for unintentional homicide

Whoever commits the offence of unintentional homicide shall be punished with the payment, of *diyyah*.

Waliyy al-damm causing death of suspect

Whoever being a *waliyy al-damm* of a deceased person causes the death of the suspect alleged to have killed the deceased shall be punished:

(a)   with imprisonment for a term of six months and shall also be liable to caning which may extend to fifty lashes if it was proved that the person killed was the one who caused the death of the deceased; or

(b)   where it was not proved that the suspect was the one who caused the death of the deceased, or it was proved that the death of the deceased was caused by the suspect but with legal justification, the *waliyy al-damm* shall be deemed to have committed intentional homicide punishable under section 200.

When intentional homicide is not punishable with death

Except in the circumstances mentioned in section 200, intentional homicide is punishable with the payment of diyyah and not with death in any of the following circumstances:

(a)   where the offender is an ascendant of the victim or where the intention of the ascendant is clearly shown to be the correction or discipline of the victim; or

(b)   where the offender, being a public servant acting for the advancement of public justice or being a person aiding a public servant so acting exceeds the powers given to him by law and necessary for the due discharge of his duty as such public servant or for assisting such public servant in the due discharge of such duty and without ill will towards the person whose death is caused; or

(c)   where the offender, in the exercise in good faith of the right of private defence of person or property, exceeds the power given to him by law and causes the death of the person against whom he is exercising such right of defence without premeditation and without any intention of doing more harm than is necessary for the purpose of such defence.

Attempts to commit intentional homicide

Whoever does any act not resulting in death with such intention or knowledge and in such circumstances that if he by that act caused death, he would be guilty of intentional homicide, shall be punished with imprisonment for a term which may extend to one year and shall also be liable to caning of one hundred lashes.

Abetment in cases of homicide

Whoever abets:

(a) any person under fifteen years of age or any insane person or any delirious person or any idiot or any person in a state of intoxication to commit suicide; or

(b) any person to commit intentional homicide or unintentional homicide; shall be punished under section 200 of this Shari'a Penal Code if:

   (i) the abettor knew of the probable or likely consequence or result or effect of the act of the persons mentioned in (a) and (b) above; and

   (ii) the execution/carrying out of the act of the persons mentioned in (a) and (b) above would not have been possible without the abetment of the abettor.

Fraudulent cancellation or destruction of document of title

Whoever fraudulently or dishonestly or with intent to cause damage or injury to the public or to any person cancels, destroys or defaces or attempts to cancel, destroy or conceals or commits theft in respect of any document which is or purports to be a document of title or a win or commits mischief in respect to any such document, shall be punished:

(a) with amputation, where the value of the title amounts to *nisab*; or

(b) in other cases, with imprisonment for a term which may extend to five years and shall also be liable to a fine.

Prohibition of *juju*

The worship or invocation of any juju shall be unlawful. Explanation: "Juju" includes the worship or invocation of any subject or being other than Allah (S.W.T.)

Offences relating to witchcraft and *juju*
Whoever:

(a) by his statement or actions represent himself to be a witch or to have the power of witchcraft; or

(b) accuses or threatens to accuse any person with being a witch or with having the power of witchcraft; or

(c) makes or sells or uses or has in his possession or represents himself to be in possession of any juju, drug or charm which is intended to be used or reported to possess the power to prevent or delay any person from doing an act which such person has a legal right to do, or to compel any person has a legal right to refrain from doing or which is alleged or reported to possess the power of causing any natural phenomenon or any disease or epidemic; or

(d) presides at or is present at or takes part in the worship or invocation of any juju which has been declared unlawful under the provisions of section 405; or

(e) is in possession of or has control over any human remains which are used or are intended to be used in connection with the worship or invocation of any juju; or

f) makes or uses or assists in making or using or has in his possession any thing whatsoever the making, use, or possession of which has been declared unlawful under the provisions of section 405 shall be punished with death.

Criminal charms
Whoever knowingly has in his possession any fetish or charm which is pretended or reputed to possess power to protect a person in the committing of any offence shall be punished with death.

NB The Kano Penal Code contains similar sections (S. 386-88), with less draconian punishments (maximum life imprisonment).

Appendix Six

Relevant provisions of the 1999 constitution

Art. 1.3 If any other law is inconsistent with the provisions of this Constitution, this Constitution shall prevail, and that other law shall, to the extent of the inconsistency, be void.

Art 4.1 The legislative powers of the Federal Republic of Nigeria shall be vested in a National Assembly for the Federation, which shall consist of a Senate and a House of Representatives.

Art 4.2 The National Assembly shall have power to make laws for the peace, order and good government of the Federation or any part thereof with respect to any matter included in the Exclusive Legislative List set out in Part I of the Second Schedule to this Constitution.

Art 4.3 The power of the National Assembly to make laws for the peace, order and good government of the Federation with respect to any matter included in the Exclusive Legislative List shall, save as otherwise provided in this Constitution, be to the exclusion of the Houses of Assembly of States.

Art. 4.4 In addition and without prejudice to the powers conferred by subsection (2) of this section, the National Assembly shall have power to make laws with respect to the following matters, that is to say:-

(a) any matter in the Concurrent Legislative List set out in the first column of Part II of the Second Schedule to this Constitution to the extent prescribed in the second column opposite thereto; and

(b) any other matter with respect to which it is empowered to make laws in accordance with the provisions of this Constitution.

Art 4.5 If any Law enacted by the House of Assembly of a State is inconsistent with any law validly made by the National Assembly, the law made by the National Assembly shall prevail, and that other Law shall, to the extent of the inconsistency, be void.

Art. 4.6 The legislative powers of a State of the Federation shall be vested in the House of Assembly of the State.

Art. 4.7 The House of Assembly of a State shall have power to make laws for the peace, order and good government of the State or any part thereof with respect to the following matters, that is to say:-

(a)   any matter not included in the Exclusive Legislative List set out in Part I of the Second Schedule to this Constitution.

(b)   any matter included in the Concurrent Legislative List set out in the first column of Part II of the Second Schedule to this Constitution to the extent prescribed in the second column opposite thereto; and

(c)   any other matter with respect to which it is empowered to make laws in accordance with the provisions of this Constitution.

Art. 4.8 Save as otherwise provided by this Constitution, the exercise of legislative powers by the National Assembly or by a House of Assembly shall be subject to the jurisdiction of courts of law and of judicial tribunals established by law, and accordingly, the National Assembly or a House of Assembly shall not enact any law, that ousts or purports to oust the jurisdiction of a court of law or of a judicial tribunal established by law.

Art. 4.9 Notwithstanding the foregoing provisions of this section, the National Assembly or a House of Assembly shall not, in relation to any criminal offence whatsoever, have power to make any law which shall have retrospective effect.

Art. 10 The Government of the Federation or of a State shall not adopt any religion as State Religion.

Art. 34.1 Every individual is entitled to respect for the dignity of his person, and accordingly —

(a)   no person shall be subject to torture or to inhuman or degrading treatment;

(b) no person shall be held in slavery or servitude; and

(c) no person shall be required to perform forced or compulsory labour.

Art. 36.12 Subject as otherwise provided by this Constitution, a person shall not be convicted of a criminal offence unless that offence is defined and the penalty therefore is prescribed in a written law, and in this subsection, a written law refers to an Act of the National Assembly or a Law of a State, any subsidiary legislation or instrument under the provisions of a law.

Art. 38.1 Every person shall be entitled to freedom of thought, conscience and religion, including freedom to change his religion or belief, and freedom (either alone or in community with others, and in public or in private) to manifest and propagate his religion or belief in worship, teaching, practice and observance.

Art. 42.1 A citizen of Nigeria of a particular community, ethnic group, place of origin, sex, religion or political opinion shall not, by reason only that he is such a person:-

(a) be subjected either expressly by, or in the practical application of, any law in force in Nigeria or any executive or administrative action of the government, to disabilities or restrictions to which citizens of Nigeria of other communities, ethnic groups, places of origin, sex, religions or political opinions are not made subject; or

(b) be accorded either expressly by, or in the practical application of, any law in force in Nigeria or any such executive or administrative action, any privilege or advantage that is not accorded to citizens of Nigeria or other communities, ethnic groups, places of origin, sex, religions or political opinions.

Art. 244.1 An appeal shall lie from decisions of a Shari'a Court of Appeal to the Court of Appeal as of right in any civil proceedings before the Shari'a Court of Appeal with respect to any question of Islamic personal law which the Shari'a Court of Appeal is competent to decide.

Art. 275.1 There shall be for any State that requires it, a Shari'a Court of Appeal for that State.

Art. 277.1 The shari'a Court of Appeal of a State shall, in addition to such other jurisdiction as may be conferred upon it by the law of the State, exercise such appellate and supervisory jurisdiction in civil proceedings involving questions of Islamic personal law which the court is competent to decide in accordance with the provisions of subsection (2) of this section.

Art. 277.2 For the purposes of subsection (1) of this section, the shari'a Court of Appeal shall be competent to decide —

(a) any question of Islamic personal law regarding a marriage concluded in accordance with that law, including a question relating to the validity or dissolution of such a marriage or a question that depends on such a marriage and relating to family relationship or the guardianship of an infant;

(b) where all the parties to the proceedings are Muslims, any question of Islamic personal law regarding a marriage, including the validity or dissolution of that marriage, or regarding family relationship, a founding or the guarding of an infant;

(c) any question of Islamic personal law regarding a *wakf*, gift, will or succession where the endower, donor, testator or deceased person is a Muslim;

(d) any question of Islamic personal law regarding an infant, prodigal or person of unsound mind who is a Muslim or the maintenance or the guardianship of a Muslim who is physically or mentally infirm; or

(e) where all the parties to the proceedings, being Muslims, have requested the court that hears the case in the first instance to determine that case in accordance with Islamic personal law, any other question.

Appendix Seven

Relevant provisions of international human rights instruments

Convention Against Torture and other Cruel, Inhuman, or Degrading Treatment or Punishment (CAT 1984):

Article 1.1:

For the purposes of this Convention, the term 'torture' means any act by which severe pain or suffering, whether physical or mental, is intentionally inflicted on a person for such purposes as obtaining from him or a third person information or a confession, punishing him for an act he or a third person has committed or is suspected of having committed, or intimidating or coercing him or a third person, or for any reason based on discrimination of any kind, when such pain or suffering is inflicted by or at the instigation of or with the consent or acquiescence of a public official or other person acting in an official capacity (...).

Article 16.1:

Each State Party shall undertake to prevent in any territory under its jurisdiction other acts of cruel, inhuman or degrading treatment or punishment which do not amount to torture as defined in Islamic criminal law 1, when such acts are committed by or at the instigation of or with the consent or acquiescence of a public official or other person acting in an official capacity (...).

International Covenant on Civil and Political Rights (ICCPR 1966)

Article 14:

All persons shall be equal before the courts and tribunals (...).

Article 26:

All persons are equal before the law (...).

The Convention on the Rights of the Child (CRC 1989):

Article 1:

For the purposes of the present Convention, a child means every human being below the age of eighteen years unless, under the law applicable to the child, majority is attained earlier.

Article 37:

States Parties shall ensure that:

No child shall be subjected to torture or other cruel, inhuman or degrading treatment or punishment. Neither capital punishment nor life imprisonment (...) shall be imposed for offences committed by persons below eighteen years of age;

Article 40:

States Parties recognise the right of every child alleged as, accused of, or recognised as having infringed the penal law to be treated in a manner consistent with the promotion of the child's sense of dignity and worth, which reinforces the child's respect for the human rights and fundamental freedom of others and which takes into account the child's age and the desirability of promoting the child's reintegration and the child's assuming a constructive role in society (...).

Differences between the Zamfara type penal codes

The Zamfara Penal Code has been adopted by five other states, viz. Bauchi, Kebbi, Jigawa, Sokoto and Yobe

Bauchi has added the definitions of Islamic Law, *Hudûd* and *Qisâs*. The punishments for the general offences (i.e. offences that are punishable under the Shari'a, but not listed in the Penal Code) (S. 92 of Zamfara Penal Code) are lower: the maximum imprisonment is one year instead of five years, the number of lashes is 40 instead of 50. The maximum fine has been increased from 5,000 Naira to 50,000 Naira. Two sections in the Zamfara Penal Code are missing in the Bauchi Penal Code: S. 191 (punishment for lurking, trespassing or housebreaking in order to commit offence punishable by imprisonment) and S. 193 (punishment for lurking, trespassing or housebreaking by night in order to commit offence punishable by imprisonment). The definition for robbery is slightly different (S. 155) The punishments for causing grievous hurt under the Bauchi Penal Code only consist of retaliation and the payment of *diya* (S. 218). The punishments in the Zamfara Penal Code also include six months of imprisonment and/or 20 lashes (S. 220). The Bauchi Penal Code includes only four sections (against seven in the Zamfara Penal Code) with regard to hurt, as in accordance with classical doctrine no distinction is made between hurt and grievous hurt nor between causing hurt and causing hurt voluntarily.

Regarding breach of official trust, Bauchi uses two sections (S. 270 and S. 271) to define breach of official trust and to define the punishments. Zamfara State has one section regarding breach of official trust, which defines both offence and punishment. The punishments vary slightly: a 15 year maximum in Bauchi and a 14 year maximum in Zamfara, and a maximum of fifty lashes in Zamfara against forty lashes in Bauchi. The Bauchi Penal Code contains an extra provision (S. 376) which prohibits singing, drumming, begging and playing cards in public places. Both the Zamfara Penal Code and the Bauchi Penal Code prohibit witchcraft, but use different definitions. The Bauchi Penal Code prohibits witchcraft and sorcery, whilst the Zamfara Penal Code prohibits witchcraft and juju (juju is not mentioned in the Bauchi Penal Code). The differences and/or similarities between juju and sorcery are unknown. The Bauchi Penal Code has only one section with regard to witchcraft (S. 404) and the Zamfara Penal Code has three (S. 405, 406, 407). Both prohibit trials by ordeal (S. 403 in the Bauchi Penal Code and S. 404 in the Zamfara Penal Code respectively).

Jigawa State has introduced exactly the same Penal Code as the State of Zamfara.

Kebbi. Unlike the Zamfara code, the Kebbi Penal Code has arranged the definitions in alphabetical order (although not entirely consistently). Moreover, there are some minor differences in this chapter. The Kebbi Penal Code lacks the definition of S. 25 in the Zamfara Penal Code (Effect) and adds the definitions of Building (S.7) and *Hudûd* (S. 52a), Regarding *zinâ* the Birnin Kebbi Penal Code has added that it can only be proven by four male witnesses (S. 127).

Sokoto. The definition of *hadd*-lashing has been added (S. 95). The definitions are presented in alphabetical order.

Yobe has added three definitions: *hudûd* (S. 57a), *qisâs* (S.57.b) and *arsh* (S.60.a).

Index